As a trainer teaching on the spiritual realm, I am excited for you to read Alisa's book written to help you understand and stand in authority over the spiritual environment around you. This book is written not as theory but from her own life story of discovering the gift of discernment, learning to understand this gift and ultimately wielding it as a weapon of war. I hope you too, while reading Alisa's book, will grow in your understanding and implementation of this amazing gift called discernment.

> —Dawna De Silva, Bethel Sozo Founder and Co-Leader, Transformation Center Overseer, Author of *Sozo: Saved, Healed, Delivered*; *Shifting Atmospheres*; *Overcoming Fear*; *Prayers, Declarations, and Strategies*; and *Warring with Wisdom*

I have had the incredible gift of a having a front row seat to Alisa's journey of loving and responding to King Jesus. She lives completely surrendered to Jesus and follows him at any cost. Her work on articulating discernment and teaching on partnering with the Holy Spirit has enriched my life and I believe it is a gift to the church. She brings a refreshing and inviting approach to daily life with God while also making plain the big theological concepts that otherwise might feel out of reach. Her persistence and her faith is inspiring, this is a must read.

> —Natasha Tunnicliffe, Worship Pastor, Church on Five

If you've ever walked into a room and thought, "Why do I suddenly feel like I've been hit by a spiritual freight train?" – this book is for you.

It's like your superpower of discernment finally got its user manual … and guess what? It's written by someone who's not just been there, but who now coaches others how to partner with Heaven and hear from God like it's a walkie-talkie from the Kingdom.

Alisa is one of our certified God Talks Coaches – which means they've been trained in the fine art of supernatural communication (and yes, we do that without a tinfoil hat or a crystal ball). She's the real deal. She brings bring humor, healing, and Holy Spirit insight all wrapped up in one glorious, glory-filled package.

The book is packed with activations, real-life stories, and those "Aha!" moments that make you go, "Oh THAT'S why I cry every time I go to Target!"

So if you've ever felt overwhelmed in public, confused by your emotions, or just really tired of people telling you you're "too sensitive," this book will not only validate your gift – it'll train you to use it like a spiritual Navy SEAL. (And coming from a former Top Gun pilot, that's saying something.)

Get the book. Read the book. Then thank me later– preferably with cookies.

Semper Fi.

>—Ed Rush, Six-time #1 bestselling author; Author of *God Talks*; F-18 Fighter Pilot (Ret.); Kingdom Strategist (Active)

RADIATING GLORY

Partnering with God Alter Atmospheres

ALISA POLKINGHORNE

Published by Alisa Polkinghorne
mitwaministries.com

First published 2025

Copyright © Alisa Polkinghorne, 2025

The moral right of the author has been asserted.

All rights reserved. Without limiting the rights under copyright restricted above, no part of this publication may be reproduced, stored in or introduced into a retrieval system, or transmitted, in any form or by any means (electronic, mechanical, photocopying, recording or otherwise), without the prior written permission of the copyright owner and publisher of this book.

Scripture quotations taken from The Holy Bible,
New International Version® NIV®
Copyright © 1973, 1978, 1984, 2011 by Biblica, Inc.
Used with permission. All rights reserved worldwide.

Scripture quotations are from The ESV® Bible
(The Holy Bible, English Standard Version®),
© 2001 by Crossway, a publishing ministry of
Good News Publishers. Used with permission.
All rights reserved.

 A catalogue record for this book is available from the National Library of Australia

ISBN: 978 1 7641483 0 6 (pbk)
ISBN: 978 1 7641483 1 3 (ebk)

Cover illustration by the author, modified by AI
Typeset by Helen Christie, Blue Wren Books
Printed and bound by Ingram Spark

To every reader who feels weighed down by the atmosphere around you, may you fall more in love with Jesus and walk confidently in your God-given authority to release the Kingdom of God.

I am so thankful for my journey with Jesus. My time at Bethel School of Supernatural Ministry enriched my life with the blessing of treasured friendships, wise mentors, and leaders who have faithfully poured into my life. I pray that *Radiating Glory* profoundly touches your heart, ignites fresh hope, and stirs you to run into the loving arms of the Father.

FOREWORD

I have known Alisa for years. I met her when she took a class I was teaching on hearing the voice of God. I had been working with the church she attended, and many of the people there had come for the same teaching. But it was when her parents enrolled in the course sometime later that I realized something very special was happening within her. A generation was shifting, and her life was a powerful beacon of the love of God that flowed so powerfully within her.

As I read this book, I can still see the powerful curiosity I first saw in her. She speaks of herself as "ever-evolving," which is what she is doing. The wisdom she now has, she wishes she had when she was much younger. How many of us can relate to this one phrase? But then I wonder what conversations I will have with her in ten years from now and if she still expresses the same wish. Alisa is a student of the Kingdom's culture, and we are all richer for her desire to learn.

Books like these are the precious gems of a person's authentic questions. They are laced with stories that lead us to greater curiosity and wonder about our own lives. Some of the stories you will relate to, some will stretch you, and others may leave you wondering if they are true. But it is here you will read how she engages with these stories and events. What was once thought impossible to her is now expressed in the way she has discovered her feelings, emotions, and encounters, all pointing to greater moments where God is waiting to be found.

Within these pages are Alisa's revelations. What she has learned has been applied; they have become her testimony. Now, her testimony has become a prophecy. I believe the greatest prophetic words that shape our lives are the ones given by the people who have been shaped by those words. This is not a theory she gives; rather it is a life expressed through the events she has witnessed.

What I love so much about how Alisa shares her story is that she knows it is her story. She invites you to discover yours. In this book, she opens her heart and allows us to see how she discovered hers. In her words, "It is when I slow down I begin to breathe deeply, calming my heart rate, seeing with greater clarity." For me, this is the secret of all secrets. In a world that strives for success that is measured by the size of our buildings, bank accounts, or five-year plans, we now have a story that is counter-cultural to all of this. She speaks of awareness and self-discovery. She speaks of being grounded and understanding your environment. She finds herself on beaches and in places to take in the beauty and wonder of the world created for us and the power of being present. In a world that celebrates our independence, she counsels interdependence. Where people crave a platform, she is happiest at a charcuterie board with friends.

Come for a journey and listen to the heart of one who seeks the Kingdom of God and longs to rest in the love and presence of Jesus. This is an ever-evolving story, and the books she writes in the future will build on the story and wisdom you hold in your hands.

Matt Beckenham
Greater Things International

CONTENTS

	Preface – Feeling the Atmosphere: Discernment	1
1.	Unmasking the Gift	7
2.	Encircled in Glory	15
3.	Unveiling Your Spiritual Authority	23
4.	The Gift Within	31
5.	Awakening Sensitivity	37
6.	Mindset Matters	41
7.	Trusting the Revealer	51
8.	Navigating Vivid Images	57
9.	Tools for Transformation	63
10.	Community	73
11.	Leadership	79
12.	Flow in the Gift	83
13.	Shifting	87
14.	The Vine and Branches	97
15.	Heart Posture	101
16.	Knowing the Father's Heart	107
	Conclusion – Heart of the Matter	113
	About the Author	117

Preface

FEELING THE ATMOSPHERE: DISCERNMENT

I did not grow up consciously aware of the spiritual realm. I knew Jesus' love for me (which is, first and foremost, the most significant life-changing message), but I didn't know the Power of God available to us all here and now. The more conversations I have had throughout my journey, the more aware I have become of the need for people to understand and talk about discernment (the recognition and interpretation of the spiritual world). If you are reading this, this may be your journey, too.

I had no idea I had the gift of discernment, let alone what to do with it.

For many, feeling an atmosphere (the surrounding influence around us) has become a pain point and more of an embarrassment than it has been a gift. Perhaps it was not a recognized gift in your circles, or you were utterly naive that you had a gift, or you needed to have the language to articulate what was happening, why it was happening, or what the purpose of it was. I have heard countless stories and many hearts longing to be understood and to learn how to utilize their gift for the Lord and His benefit. My desire is for Saints like you to be inspired, encouraged, and reignited with a passion to see the Lord move in Power across the earth.

Abba Father places good gifts in our hands; the Holy Spirit then teaches us how to use that gift. As we learn to trust in Him, the more we engage with the gift that He has given us, the more He trusts us with increased authority.

> *There are different kinds of gifts, but the same Spirit distributes them. There are different kinds of service, but the same Lord. There are different kinds of working, but in all of them and everyone it is the same God at work. Now to each one, the manifestation of the Spirit is given for the common good. To one there is given through the Spirit a message of wisdom, to another a message of knowledge by means of the same Spirit, to another faith by the same Spirit, to another gifts of healing by that one Spirit, to another miraculous powers, to another prophecy, to another distinguishing between spirits, to another speaking in different kinds of tongues, and to still another the interpretation of tongues. All these are the work of one and the same Spirit, and he distributes them to each one, just as he determines* (1 Corinthians 12:4–11 NIV).

There is something so beautiful about stewarding what the Lord has placed in our hands. As we respond in faith, partnering with Him, we will ultimately see it grow, which is where I am today. I have the gift of distinguishing between Spirits. My learning has sometimes felt clumsy because I often had no idea what to do with it or tried to work it out independently rather than turning to the All-knowing Lord of all and the beautiful people around me.

I imagine it like receiving a simple children's version of a toy. As we spend time with it, we receive upgrades; additional pieces are added regularly, and over time, the toy becomes more complex, requiring deeper insight and a stronger connection with its Creator to use it as intended. We steward the talents in our hands, and our Creator expands our knowledge and understanding of what we have been faithful with. Yet, in the same breath, it really isn't about us but Him, the Giver of the gift, by grace, who works through us. It baffles me that He really doesn't need us, and yet it is His delight to have connection and intimacy with His children, co-laboring with us, centering us into fellowship with the King of Kings.

My journey has not been linear where the Lord has revealed wisdom, and that's it; there's nothing more to be done, but it is an ever-evolving process. I went from discerning (feeling) what one person felt to what was occurring corporately in a room to regionally, then nationally. Each time, I would ask the Lord, whom I had the privilege of interceding on behalf of. Some days, the Holy Spirit would give me a name; other times, various images, such as a room or even a map, indicating the region or nation. I partnered with Heaven to intercede or engage in conversation with individuals who had been highlighted. I believe my prayers carry authority and power; something must happen in the spiritual realm every time I pray. There is a shift because of the power of the name in which I am praying. There is power in the name of Jesus.

I wish I had been aware of discernment in my early years and had the tools I have now in my walk with the Lord. He has taught me to be faithful to what is in my hand and to consider it a gift to feel what is in an atmosphere. I can choose what I do with it: to bury and ignore it, to recognize it and do nothing, or to steward it, be faithful, and to respond and see it increase.

Are you longing to utilize discernment as a life-giving weapon? To partner with the Holy Spirit and walk intimately with Him? To be enlightened about the gifts He has given you and how to utilize those gifts personally.

I am sharing this glimpse into my own experiences and understanding of the atmosphere to encourage and inspire you to press in, seek understanding for yourself, and become attentive and self-aware of your own emotions, thoughts, behaviors, and belief systems.

I believe divine realignment is happening. The church is recalibrating to the heartbeat of Heaven. We are called living sacrifices; our lives are that of worship, a sweet incense to the Lord. We are to give Him the glory in all things in our everyday moments. We hear the whispers in our hearts to approach a stranger and love them, to be a listening ear or a shoulder to cry on. Whispers of love, taking the opportunity to have vulnerable conversations, to seek reconciliation in a relationship. God is always speaking of love, grace, mercy, forgiveness, reconciliation, and restoration.

Shift in Current World Atmospheres

The atmosphere during COVID-19 felt heavy, with an overwhelming sense of fear, confusion, insecurity, anxiety, depression, uncertainty, disappointment, sadness, grief, anger, and even desperation. You may have felt a myriad of these emotions for yourself or may have recognized when others felt that way. The season was painful, and for many, it was full of loss and heartbreak.

Yet it was a season of divine shake-up for the body of Christ. This shake-up realigned our priorities, our relationships, and our families, bringing about a recalibration of what our lives look like.

I believe it is time for us to rise up above the clutter. We have a responsibility as the body of Christ to respond to the call of God, to love as Jesus loved, to live as Jesus lived, and to see light obliterate darkness. It is time for lovers of Jesus to arise for such a time as this. To bring peace where there is fear, clarity in confusion, hope for the hopeless, and identity for the lost, broken, and insecure. Our commission is to usher in the Kingdom of God, releasing hope, life, peace, and joy. One way we can do this is through intercession and the gift of discernment.

Here are my experiences with discernment. I have seen people profoundly touched as I have partnered with the Lord to see the Kingdom of God invade Earth.

Intentionality

This book is intentionally written to connect you, the spiritually sensitive Christian burdened by the atmosphere around you, with the gift of discernment you possess. It empowers you to use that gift as it was intended: to glorify God and set the captives free. I am drawing from my own journey of discovering this gift in the hope that what I have experienced transforms you from feeling weighed down, confused, and anxious in public spaces to walking confidently with influence and tangible power, ultimately bringing light to obliterate darkness.

This book provides practical tools and activations for using discernment as a life-giving weapon while growing in intimacy with Jesus, encouraging you to know you are walking within the glory realm, breaking off small thinking, limitations, hopelessness, and powerlessness.

Each chapter concludes with an *Activation* point, a time to *Linger and Listen* to the Spirit, and a moment to encounter God by *Asking Jesus*. I desire that all who read this book will fall more in love with Jesus and walk in their God-given authority to release the Kingdom of God.

Activation: Dream with God about what it could look like to believe for entire towns, cities, and nations to encounter the Lord in a moment.

Linger and Listen: You may hear a word, see an image or color, be brought back to a memory, have a song playing in your head or a Scripture, etc. It may seem random, but press in, linger a little longer, and write it down; treasure what He says over you. He is always speaking.

Ask Jesus: Ask the Godhead (Father, Son, Holy Spirit) you are most comfortable with: How do you see me? What do you love about me? Who do you say that I am? Where are you in the room? Spend time in intimacy, in adoration and praise, telling the Lord what you love about Him.

Chapter 1

UNMASKING THE GIFT

I see an image of a door slightly opened. Curiosity and hunger to discover more stir within me as I peep through. A door just waiting to be pushed wide open to walk hand-in-hand with the Holy Spirit. Our life is a divine dance with the King of Kings as we fix our gaze on Him amidst all the distractions the world throws at us. Discernment is a sweet gift that enables us to see beyond the situation or person to what is happening in the spiritual realm. You see, there is a gold key in your hand waiting to be used; it is a key to release the fruits of the spirit to a lost and broken world. I am confident that we have been fully equipped to utilize discernment as a life-giving weapon. It is an opportunity to recognize what the Lord is revealing and to partner with Him and see God's power demonstrated.

What if we believe that entire towns, cities, and nations could encounter the Lord in a moment? What if we understood that as the body of Christ, we can see this in our lifetime? My heart is passionately stirred more than ever to see His Kingdom come and to see many lives profoundly touched by the God that is love, peace, hope, and joy. The Spirit of the Sovereign Lord is upon us, an Isaiah 61 mandate for us as believers. We have the tools to set captives free!

The Spirit of the Sovereign Lord is on me because the Lord has anointed me to proclaim good news to the poor. He has sent me to bind up the brokenhearted, to proclaim freedom for the captives and release from darkness for the prisoners, to proclaim the year of the Lord's favor and the day of vengeance of our God, to comfort all who mourn, and provide for those who grieve in Zion – to bestow on them a crown of beauty instead of ashes, the oil of joy instead of mourning, and a garment of praise instead of a spirit of despair. They will be called oaks of righteousness, a planting of the Lord to display his splendor (Isaiah 61:1–3 NIV).

We have the Holy Spirit to enable us to discern the brokenhearted, captives, prisoners, those mourning, grieving, and oppressed by the Spirit of despair. The Spirit of the Sovereign Lord is on us! We have the privilege of releasing hope, joy, life, peace, and freedom, bringing the light, proclaiming the Lord's favor, and placing on a crown of beauty and a garment of praise. I believe this is a mandate for the Bride!

How It All Started

Ministry school is where I gained the knowledge that I had the gift of discernment and began learning about shifting the atmosphere. I recall that first week. Hundreds of students filled the auditorium. The anxiety and nervousness were so high I could feel it in the air. It was so unbearable for me that I had to escape. So I left school very abruptly, practically running out of the room. I began to question what I had done. Had I made a huge mistake? I moved to the other side of the world to attend ministry school, and now everything in me wanted to drive home, pack up my bags, and fly back to Australia. It was all too overwhelming. Prior to being in the auditorium, I had felt so different. You see, I woke up excited. I love adventure and embracing new challenges. There was an anticipation in my spirit to do something I had never done – move overseas, meet new people, and study at ministry school. I was so full of expectation when I arrived; nothing in me felt anxious, nervous, or scared but rather a thrill of adrenaline. Yet the moment I stepped into that room, it was as though I plunged into a pool of doubt and fear, questioning and anxiety. Once I left the auditorium, I thought, *How had things changed so quickly? Why was I so consumed? What had caused such a dramatic shift in a moment?*

I had no language or understanding of this, but it brought me back to previous events in my life where I had felt the same. Events in which I chose to leave, feeling unwell and not quite myself, which I often associated with needing more introverted time. In fact, so many times in my life, I have put my experiences of discernment down to not having rested enough or spent enough time alone. It was a stark contrast, and I had to get to the bottom of it. I chose to go back to the auditorium and talk to my mentor. As he approached me, he could see I was not okay. "You have the gift of discernment. I have it, too, to be able to discern emotions, feeling them in our body." He articulated everything I had perceived that day; doubting whether I should have come, feeling fearful, anxious, nervous, and out of place. For a moment, I was speechless. How did he know this?

I was picking up the emotions of the people around me, the feelings of others in the room, the spiritual atmosphere. This perceiving varies from person-to-person, but some, as I do, tangibly experience it through mind and body—things just feel "off".

It was the beginning of my journey, exploring what it meant to have the gift of discernment. No one ever explained this to me before. I knew what it was like to feel out of control, immersed immediately into internal chaos. I had experienced it my whole life. I never knew this was a gift or what to do when I distinguished an emotion or a thought that did not align with what I felt or thought in the moment.

Memories flashed, one after another, before my eyes as I recalled one experience after the next. How often had I felt the environment, thinking something was seriously wrong with me? How could one person go from excitement to crushing pain in the blink of an eye? I saw these experiences now from a completely different perspective, and it just took one person, one explanation. It got me thinking. How many people have lived their lives believing they were unstable and in chaos, unknowingly having the gift of discernment, believing those emotions and thoughts were their own? A roulette reel of spinning thoughts and feelings, constantly changing with each person they encountered. Oh, and the upheaval of emotions entering another city or nation!

Knowing I am able to recognize when there is an immediate and dramatic shift in my thoughts and emotions has profoundly impacted my life. I now live with stability, not in chaos or feeling out of control within minutes of entering a new environment or encountering others. But rather, recognizing what is happening, what I am discerning in an environment, fixing my gaze upon the Lord, and releasing the Fruits of the Spirit.

As my mind is fixed on truth, my metron affects those around me. Kris Valloton defines metron in his book *Spirit Wars*, "The

Greek word metron means our place of influence or sphere of authority."

If the living God lives in me, the fruits of the Spirit are readily available. I am in union with God; Him in me and I in Him, so that the fruits of the Spirit are my reality. I choose to have my mind conscious of what I carry and to release love, joy, peace, patience, kindness, goodness, faithfulness, gentleness, and self-control.

Whether conscious or subconscious, we release what we believe about ourselves. If we believe we are lovable, we will be loved, and the same goes for the opposite: If we believe we are rejectable, we will often be rejected. I know this concept may seem wild to you, but watch it unfold before your eyes.

Belief Systems

We must choose to live intentionally, believing we have the Spirit of the Living God dwelling inside us. As we meet people each day, they will encounter the living God and recognize the fruits of the Spirit **through the belief in what we carry**.

Entering a room, I have often had colleagues, families, even students approach me and say, "I feel so much joy when I am around you." The joy I carried affected everyone in my presence. As a mentor of mine always says, "You leak what you carry." Whatever is in us flows out of us.

You know those people in your life who are a "breath of fresh air." Yes, absolutely personality plays a part, but what if it was significantly more than that? What if everyone chose to know that they, too, bring a tangible change to the atmosphere with a mind that is set on the truth? To be that breath of fresh air that releases the Kingdom of God everywhere you go. You can consciously choose to focus on the Kingdom of God, to be the light of the world and to be the radical change in every atmosphere that you are in, pray over, or think about.

You have more authority and power than you know: the authority that Jesus claimed when He died for us. It is authority *from* God, *for* God's glory. Abba Father longs for us to step up, walk in faith, and accept the authority He paid for; to take risks, and partner with him to see His Kingdom come.

God longs to encounter His children, to remove their heavy burdens. Jesus sees his children tormented by the lies and schemes of the enemy where there is destruction, chaos, anxiety, confusion, and pain. Jesus paid the price so the entire world could be set free.

Unacceptable

We do not think it strange in today's society for people to be captive to fear, anxiety, and depression. And this is so heartbreaking! I have encountered powerlessness all around me. Statements like, "Well, it is what it is," simply accepting things the way that they are. For too long the Saints have settled with anxiety, calling it the "thorn in their side," their portion. Somewhere along the way it has become accepted to be bound by chains, shackles, or to have knives protruding out of our backs. The sheer Power and brilliance of Abba Father changes everything. Resurrection Power is available for God's children to be set free from strongholds that have bound society for too long.

Freedom is available; it is ours if we choose to take it. You are equipped, and you have been empowered to see tangible change in your life. It starts with a choice, a decision to be that change.

The importance of the renewed mind is explicitly stated in Romans:

> *Do not be conformed to this world, but be transformed by the renewal of your mind, that by testing you may discern what is the will of God, what is good and acceptable and perfect will* (Romans 12:2 ESVUK).

We must renew our minds and in the renewing, we can test and discern the will of God. As we align our minds with Him, the overflow is the product of our mindsets. The Lord is the Prince of Peace and He resides in us! As we rewire our minds, allowing the Holy Spirit to reveal His heavenly perspective, our normal is now the Kingdom, for the Kingdom of God lives in us. Anything else is trespassing and has no place in us. Jesus is the life-giver. His name has all authority, power, and dominion. Everything must-and will bow down to Yahweh.

We have the privilege to partner with Heaven and shift individual lives as well as entire atmospheres. By becoming aware of what individuals are carrying or what we are picking up in the spiritual atmosphere, *we have the authority to shift it*. There is power in the name of Jesus. Darkness must bow to light. Anxiety must bow to the Prince of Peace. We have a responsibility and must play a part in imparting Truth and Life into every situation. When we enter a conversation, rather than being overcome by the heaviness that someone is feeling, we can choose to pray and release the opposite. To see them leave a conversation feeling completely different from when they entered it.

Activation: Jesus loves you so much that He wants to take the burdens that you are carrying and put them on His shoulders, nailed to the cross. Read Romans 12:2. Sit down with Jesus and allow Him to reveal belief systems that are not aligned with God's heart. There is an opportunity for a divine exchange. Imagine holding the lie in your hand, giving it to Jesus, and asking Him to take it and reveal the truth.

Linger and Listen: In your imagination picture the golden key in your hand waiting to be used; it is a key to release the fruits of the Spirit to a lost and broken world. Cultivate within yourself an awareness of Immanuel (God with us) light, peace, joy, and hope. Become aware of God's nearness and allow His presence to tangibly encounter you.

Ask Jesus: Ask the Lord, " Is there anything I am holding onto that I need to give back to you today?" Ask Him for divine strategies.

Chapter 2

ENCIRCLED IN GLORY

I had a vision once that profoundly impacted my life and the way that I interact with the world. The results were as if Heaven was overshadowing me.

I was in an old library, standing on the top rung of a ladder that was leaning against a floor-to-ceiling bookshelf. As I was reaching up to take a book from the shelf, I heard a racket coming from the entrance of the library. Mothers and children were screaming as a man dressed in black from head to toe, with a balaclava on his head and a gun in his hand, burst in. He ran, looking around with the intention of finding someone. He headed to the back of the library where I was situated. He stopped with a clear view of me standing on the ladder. Looking directly down the aisle, he pointed his gun at me and began to shoot. I had no idea who he was, but he was furious and on a mission to take me down. Amazingly, I felt so calm the entire time and began to laugh, which, of course, made him angrier. As he shot, the bullets flew toward me, immediately stopping in midair. I watched as each bullet hovered in front of my body and then dropped to the ground. The man stared at his gun as though it were faulty. As quickly as he entered the library, he ran off in a huff as though both frustrated and fearful.

I asked the Lord to show me why the bullets stopped in front of me and dropped to the ground. Immediately, I saw the hedge of protection around me in the form of a blue, shimmering Dome. You see, when the bullets touched the Dome they ceased in their tracks. The Lord said, "No harm will come to you."

Living Under the Dome

The Glory Dome became more than just a vision. As I asked the Holy Spirit about this Dome of protection, I engaged all of my senses, visualizing being inside of it. His presence was weighty yet peaceful. It felt light, bringing rest and stillness to my mind and heart. It smelled of the most delightfully sweet fragrance of cherry blossoms. His voice whispered truth and grace to me, in love, like rejuvenating waves rolling over me on a calm ocean day. I could taste honey and sweetness. It was ecstatic and oh-so-wonderful, delighting all of my senses!

This vision has altered the trajectory of how I now live. I am a walking glory realm, yet so are you. It has become a refuge for me. If everything within this blue shimmering Dome represents the Kingdom of God, what would life look like? The fruits of the Holy Spirit would be evident in all we do. As we press in and fixate on the Lord's face, we will recognize lies and those belief systems misaligned with God's heart, calling people around us higher. Faith is increased and tangible, and we are filled with a longing to see the impossible made possible. The Glory Dome releases within its wake signs, wonders, and miracles; the spiritual world flooding into the natural. We pray, "Your Kingdom come on Earth as it is in Heaven," and so, have the privilege of ushering in the Kingdom of God.

As I envisioned this Dome of protection around me, I was reminded of the promises of God. The Lord brought to mind the many testimonies of people being protected, such as being shot at, yet the bullets missing them entirely. I think of it much like the Iron Dome in Israel. I heard about it from a lady who lived in Israel and saw a missile launched, heading straight to where she was standing, but in midair, it shifted its course one hundred and eighty degrees and landed in the Mediterranean Sea.

The Dome of Protection is a supernatural force having a natural impact on the people around it. The safety is not in the Dome itself but in the One who promises protection, the maker of Heaven and Earth, the One who fights on our behalf.

I believe this hedge of protection (shield of faith) is a tangible reality for each person to interact with. The moment I had this vision, I engaged my faith, envisioning how this reality affects not only the spiritual realm but the natural realm as well. Ephesians 6 describes the armor of God we are to put on daily.

Take up the shield of faith, with which you can extinguish all the flaming arrows of the evil one (Ephesians 6:16 NIV).

As children of God, we have been commanded to take up the shield of faith which "extinguishes all the flaming arrows." To grow in faith, we must grow in trust, in connection, in dependency, in belief in who God is and what He can do. It requires a daily posture of communing with God in worship, being immersed in and meditating on the Word of God, and engaging with the Spirit of Truth, allowing this time to arrest our attention and our affection to the One that we love.

In fact, *without faith, it's impossible to please God* (Hebrews 10:6 NIV).

Thus, I began picturing the Dome in my everyday life. What would it look like to consciously live with that Dome of protection around me? I had an atmosphere in me and around me that was stronger than the atmosphere of this world; the knowledge that the Holy Spirit lives in me, envelopes me, and all that I do in union with Christ. I am one with the Lord God Almighty.

Living in Awareness

We all have a responsibility to take up our shield of faith daily, confident that the fiery arrows are extinguished in the presence of the living God. I believe everyone has a Dome around them. What if we lived with the awareness that *He who is in me is greater than he who is in the world*? (1 John 4:4).

In my journey of discerning an atmosphere, I can choose to become overwhelmed by what I am sensing or I can choose to shift it. I visualize the Dome, fix my gaze on the things above and watch as my Dome (the Lord) releases the frequency of Heaven and a wave of love and peace, touching everyone in its wake. I imagine this like a rock that is thrown into the center of a still lake creating a constant flow of ripples, endless capillary waves, pulsating throughout the atmosphere, impacting everything it touches.

Have you ever noticed when you walk past someone, even complete strangers, and are suddenly drawn to them maybe by a feeling of safety, peace, acceptance, or the complete opposite, where you immediately want to avoid that person at all costs, from feelings of fear, anger, rejection? Every day, we encounter things that seem to be subconscious responses, it's just what we "do." The more I have chosen to be aware of this, the more

I realize the impact we all have on the people around us, either for the positive or the negative. We all have our own metron that determines the way people around us experience us. What if we chose to continually renew our minds to focus on the things above and watch as it profoundly touches the lives of everyone along our path?

This brings me back to The Dome. We all have a sphere of influence and can determine who we are, and how those around us experience us due to the belief systems we have.

Whatever we behold, we become. We get to determine our life and our own realities either choosing to do it on our own or choosing to do it in partnership with the Holy Spirit. The Lord is the one who renews our minds and reveals truth, insights, and revelation. Jesus is my measuring stick whilst simultaneously being the One who sanctifies my mind and teaches me the ways of the Kingdom. Nothing can be done in the absence of intimacy with the Lord. We can try all we want to conjure up our reality and will see changes in our world and perspective, but how much greater if we seek wisdom from Him and see Him transform our lives for the best?

See Your Dome of Protection

Picturing the Dome for me, is a tool that always leads me immediately to the Holy Spirit, to be attentive to the spiritual atmosphere around me and be led by the All-Knowing one; He is the Way, the Truth, and the Life. As we take up our shield of faith, we realign to the reality that we are currently seated in Heavenly places. As we take up the shield of faith, the worries of this world fade and we recalibrate our perspectives, our beliefs, our thoughts, and feelings back into alignment with how our loving Father views us and our circumstances.

I recall a time I was in the grocery store with a friend of mine. The moment we entered the store, I was hit with a wall of heaviness. Immediately, a weariness came over me; it was tiring to walk and shop. I even felt slightly dizzy and anxious, and confusion came over me, along with a wave of nausea. I wanted to leave the store immediately. I hadn't felt like this outside of the store. In fact, I was full of energy and peace, and I was excited to complete my shopping. As we stood in the line, we talked about what we were feeling. I shared how I often pictured the Dome. I encouraged her to ask the Holy Spirit what her Dome looked like and engage with the Lord to see what she carried and was to release into the store. As we partnered with the Holy Spirit, His presence came on us so strongly. No longer were we experiencing feelings of heaviness, but rather as if something had lifted and we both felt lighter, filled with joy and peace, and began laughing. Where there was heaviness just seconds earlier, we felt the shift, and it disappeared. This is what I believe we are meant to do everywhere we go.

The Dome is a tool enabling us to be in step with the Holy Spirit, releasing Heaven on Earth as we go about our day. There is something so powerful when we live a life that seeks to reveal Jesus in all that we do. If Jesus healed all who came to Him, what would it look like to believe that anyone who entered your Dome experienced healing, deliverance, freedom, love, and life and was met with compassion, understanding, and peace? Old mindsets are challenged as those around me are called to a higher belief system, no longer victims but empowered to thrive. Those who encounter the Dome are set free from anxiety, depression, chronic illness, and confusion. All receive fresh visions and dreams for their lives, restored hope, and the knowledge of how loved and seen they are. Those encountering your Dome, enslaved by demonic possession and oppression, are set free, and those entities fleeing as darkness is eradicated.

So, the Dome is an essential tool for seeing the impossibilities with God become realities.

Activation: Close your eyes and engage all your senses as you imagine your Shield of Faith or Hedge of Protection. What colors, shapes, or images do you see? What does it feel like as you sense His presence on and around you? What does it sound like? What does it smell like? What does it taste like? Visualization has helped me become conscious of the presence of God in my midst.

Linger and Listen: As you practice this daily, atmospheres will shift, and realms will be revealed in the everyday world around you. Describe the Glory realm of God. Become attentive to the spiritual atmosphere around you and allow Him to speak.

Ask Jesus: Ask the Holy Spirit to uncloak facets of His nature and character and how they are experienced in your own Dome. Allow Him to speak through Scripture of what your life could look like through His Kingdom realities.

Chapter 3

UNVEILING YOUR SPIRITUAL AUTHORITY

For our struggle is not against flesh and blood, but against the rulers, against the authorities, against the powers of this dark world, and against the spiritual forces of evil in the heavenly realms (Ephesians 6:12 NIV).

Discernment is a gift from God and manifests itself in a variety of ways. My focus here is on feeling what is in an atmosphere and warring to see that atmosphere move. The emphasis is not on judgment, in seeing the pain or bondage of someone else, but rather on knowing the God who sets people free. It is partnering with Him, shifting the atmosphere with the spiritual authority given to you, while bringing glory, honor, and praise, always back to God. This gift we have been given; to recognize the spiritual forces of evil and the powers of darkness, is well beyond what we see, feel, and experience in the natural world but a discerning of the spiritual realm and partnering with Jesus, the victorious One. It is Jesus Christ that sets free! *So if the Son sets you free, you will be free indeed (*John 8:36 NIV).

Scriptural Foundation

Hebrews 5 mentions the roles of those who are mature in Christ and use what they have experienced to distinguish or discern what is good and evil.

> *But solid food is for the mature, whose spiritual senses perceive heavenly matters. And they have been adequately trained by what they've experienced to emerge with an understanding of the difference between what is truly excellent and what is evil and harmful* (Hebrews 5:14 TPT).

What if I told you this doesn't stop with simply knowing the atmosphere and what people are carrying into it? We also have the responsibility to respond to it. We have a choice to walk in the authority that has been given to us as Co-heirs with Christ, for He delights in co-laboring with us. We pray regularly in the Lord's prayer: "Your Kingdom come, and your will be done on earth as it is in Heaven." His Kingdom is here, now, and we have the privilege of working with Him to see it revealed on Earth as it is in Heaven. Imagine intentionally bringing Heaven to Earth. Seeing darkness and all associated with it obliterated and restored the Kingdom of Light. Imagine lives restored in a moment that every individual you encounter in a day is set free, saved, healed, and delivered. The very Power that raised Jesus from the dead lives in us.

We have been equipped and empowered with all that we need to thrive and see those around us thrive, too.

For much of my life, I lived like a victim of this world. I avoided going to events or places like a cafe, a hotel, or the grocery store because I knew how I would feel when I arrived – heavy and weighed down. I would start out feeling full of peace, excitement, and joy, but in a matter of minutes, become so overcome with anxiety, like being trapped inside a cage, frantically attempting to get out. There was nothing I could do. I allowed my environment to overwhelm me. I convinced myself it was wise to simply forgo those places and steer clear of specific people. Some people were simply more exhausting than others; zapping energy from me the moment I began communicating with them. I became completely depleted and ready for a nap. Much of my life was spent evading those people for extended periods of time for the sake of my health and wellbeing. Little did I know that choice had an impact not only on me but the individual and the environment itself.

What if I had missed an opportunity to bring joy, light, and peace?

I am reminded of David in the book of Samuel. Both 1 Samuel and Acts describe David as a 'Man after God's own heart.' As David was about to fight Goliath, he made a declaration:

> *David said to the Philistine, "You come against me with sword and spear and javelin, but I come against you in the name of the LORD Almighty, the God of the armies of Israel, whom you have defied ... All those gathered here will know that it is not by sword or spear that the LORD saves; for the battle is the LORD's, and he will give all of you into our hands"* (1 Samuel 17:45, 47 NIVUK).

David knew that He could take on the giant that everyone else was fearful of. He was confident as he faced Goliath, *because David knew his authority* was not what he could do but what the Lord could do through Him. He wasn't fearful as he had an intimate history with God where he had faced and triumphed over wild animals as a shepherd protecting his sheep. He was faithful as he trained up and acknowledged that it was the Lord who rescued him (verse 37).

David knew that when He fought, the Lord Almighty was with him. He ensured that everyone would hear God was on His side. David cultivated a life of worship to the Lord. His worship did not start when he was invited into the room to play for Saul. He played musical instruments, sang, danced, built the temple, and dedicated it to the Lord. Stewarding the presence; David poured his heart out in thoughts, words, and actions. His heart was moved by God's heart, affectionately and passionately pursuing the One he loved. He had a personal history with the Lord. With his God-given authority built in the secret place, he shifted atmospheres. God longs for us to lovingly pursue Him with our hearts focused on beholding the One we love.

In Chapter 16, we read that Saul had an evil spirit that tormented him. Saul's attendants had the insight to find someone who could play the lyre. They discerned that there was an evil spirit, and the atmosphere had to shift.

> *Whenever the spirit from God came on Saul, David would take up his lyre and play. Then relief would come to Saul; he would feel better, and the evil spirit would leave him* (1 Samuel 16:23 NIV).

I can imagine that many people would not voluntarily enter a room where an evil spirit is tormenting someone, yet, there was David, faithfully playing worship music. It was in the worship that the atmosphere shifted, and the evil spirit left. Evil had a hold on Saul, yet the atmosphere shifted in the presence of David playing. I believe it was not the lyre that drove the evil spirit to flee, but rather, it was the presence of a worshipper. He was a man after God's heart, prioritizing and stewarding the presence of the living God in all that he did and everywhere he went.

Our heart's attention and affection matters. We, too, carry authority as we are with the Lord God Almighty, to enter into atmospheres and watch as those tormented are set free in the presence of God.

Choosing Right

I have missed divine appointments to be the light in the darkness by my choices to avoid unnerving situations and people. I am not saying that the responsibility rests solely on my shoulders to shift an atmosphere, but I must prioritize, worshiping with an awareness of the presence of the One living inside of me. It is an opportunity to positively impact the environment around me and watch as the demonic flee.

What if being overwhelmed by an environment did not need to be our reality anymore? Instead, we are given the choice to bring the atmosphere of the Kingdom of God. We can walk confidently and boldly with our heads held high, knowing that we are victorious in Christ and that there is nothing left to fear. We do not need to be scared or intimidated by discerning the atmosphere around us.

What would it look like if the body of Christ was so confident in their identity in Jesus that they stepped into places of darkness and pain, places that typically scare people and are usually avoided? To confidently release the Kingdom of light and live full of boldness, and courage.

This is a call to be bold and not shrink back but rather, take action.

It no longer needs to feel intimidating or too much to handle because the God of the Universe is on your side. We have the cloud of witnesses cheering us on every step of the way and ministering angels specifically assigned to us individually.

Rightness Begins with Jesus

When I gave my life to Jesus, He took my sin, washed me as white as snow, and called me righteous and holy. Through Jesus' death and resurrection, all of us are given life, hope, and a future. The moment we give our lives to Jesus we are no longer separated but restored back to the original design where we have access to pure intimacy with Abba Father, rid of sin, guilt, shame, and condemnation. We are given a helper, a counselor, our ever-present help in the Holy Spirit. We are given power from on high. Jesus told us it would be better that He should go. It is better, for we now have the Holy Spirit, the Living God living inside of us. Our bodies are the temples, the Tabernacle, the Holy of Holies carrying the reverent, holy, majestic God in us through the gift of the Holy Spirit.

Oh how beautiful grace is, a gift undeserved! We never earned it, and could never work for it but we are forgiven, made spotless, restored, and called children of God.

I am utterly convinced that Jesus' love is tangible. It must impact the atmosphere as we walk in union with Him. Spiritual forces are at work in and around us at all times. Having the gift to discern spiritual atmospheres and the authority to shift them enables us to partner with the King of Glory and see the Kingdom of God advance in our midst.

So let us choose to take our authority, shift the atmosphere, looking to the All-Powerful One, the Maker of Heaven and Earth, calling on the name of Jesus Christ. For He joyfully chooses to partner with us, His beloved children.

Activation: Spend some time meditating on the story of David and Goliath in 1 Samuel 17:45–50. Ask the Holy Spirit to reveal an area where fear and intimidation have robbed you. Ask for a prophetic act to partner with Jesus to see Life released into the situation.

Linger and Listen: What is His response to you? Wait on Holy Spirit to speak to you.

Ask Jesus: "What would it look like to be so assured of my identity in you, that darkness flees in my presence?"

Chapter 4

THE GIFT WITHIN

Growing up, the emotions I felt, and the thoughts I had were like a pendulum swing, ranging from one extreme emotion to the next. When I was alone I felt stable, peaceful, full of joy and happiness. Emotions intensified when I was surrounded by crowds of people. I never really enjoyed shopping malls or crowded places, and could never articulate why. I honestly believed that my mind was on a wild journey and I couldn't navigate how to be in control of it. Caught in the swirl and confusion, full of energy, then instantly so incredibly tired and worn out. I would ask myself, "How do others keep their emotions at bay? How is it possible to feel this many feelings in such a short period of time? Why am I only aware of my emotions when I am in public, surrounded by crowds of people? Is everyone else this messed up?" It created internal turmoil as I forged my way through the inconsistent, unpredictable emotions that would come upon me at any time or place.

The contrast of extremes scared me. I would feel happiness, excitement, anticipation, and, in an instant, feel a huge spectrum of opposite emotions of hopelessness, despair, heartbreak, anxiety, depression, anger, and even thinking suicidal thoughts – all within a matter of minutes. These were not limited to feelings. Vivid images would flood my mind as I walked past certain people. Over time, I chose to harden my heart and numb my emotions completely.

Not My Normal

Once I attended a birthday celebration. I was excited to see old friends, reminisce on decades of memories together, and dream about the future. Socializing is one of my favorite things to do. At this particular celebration, I was surrounded by dear friends I had known for a long time. They were so familiar, comfortable, and safe to me. As we gathered around the charcuterie board, it hit me. A surge of emotions, uncontrollable and unexpected. My heart raced, my eyes darted around the room. Fear and anxiety overcame me in an instant. I had lost my ability to socialize. Where do I put my hands? Where do I look? What do I talk about? Who do I talk to? I'd forgotten how to communicate and became consumed with worry. Things grew heavier; my body felt hot and clammy; I grew lethargic and dizzy. I began questioning the value of my life and if my presence was even needed on earth.

Outwardly, I looked put together, but inwardly, I was in turmoil. This was not my normal, in fact, I had not felt anything like it with such intensity. "Lord, what am I feeling?" I prayed. The Holy Spirit spoke so intimately, drawing my attention to individual people. As He highlighted one friend in the room, the all-consuming feelings subsided. I looked at them. The pain I experienced was now less intense, but my mind was in a confusing fog; everything was a blur, and the words spoken were hard to understand. The Lord then highlighted a second person but the feeling was slightly different: a tightness in my chest – a struggle to breathe, fear and insecurity flooding my thoughts such as, *I don't belong here; No one notices me, I should never have come. I don't even know how to have a normal conversation. Please don't ask me a question.* A spiral of thoughts swirled in my mind. Then, as my eyes were drawn to the third person, depressed thoughts and a horrific image of suicide flooded my mind.

Seeing the three different friends in the room, I came to realize that what I had felt was a glimpse of what each friend was feeling. When all three people were highlighted to me, I felt a combination of the emotions I had just encountered in isolation all at once. It was overwhelming, consuming, and more than what I could handle. I needed to escape. I got up abruptly and ran out the front door.

In the front yard, I stood doubled over with my hands on my knees in an attempt to catch my breath. What had just happened? Why did it happen? What was I feeling? My heart was broken. Could people I love really be going through such turbulence and pain without me even being aware of it until now? Why were my eyes drawn to different friends as I felt, thought, and saw different images in my mind? Why was it highlighted to me, and why then?

A flood of questions and confusion swept over me like a tidal wave. I was not sure what to do with this knowledge but kept it to myself along with the heartbreak. I knew this was shown to me purposely, it wasn't by accident.

This was the first time such an experience was so clear and tangible to me. I began to understand I had picked up on the atmosphere. It felt so real to me that I struggled to distinguish between what I had thought and felt and what my reality truly was. It was so unusual and out of the blue. My whole being was affected as I experienced both psychological and physiological responses in my mind and body. I did not have language for it then, but I knew that the Lord was so intentional in highlighting each person individually and allowing me to feel something unique each time.

Carrying the Gift

Years have passed since then, but now I know this is not uncommon; many have had such experiences, and I am thankful for my journey of discovery and being able to share it with you.

As you read this, you may recall times that you have experienced an emotion or thought that was not familiar to you. You may have had a thought which caused you to think, *that was strange,* or *I wonder why that popped into my mind?* How many of us have had similar experiences but have not had anyone to explain or share insights as to why this was happening? You see, I share my experience with the intention to bring clarity to the spiritual gifts in your life.

A year after this experience, I learned that I carried a gift called discernment, a gift in which I perceived the feelings and thoughts of others around me. A gift where I could pick up what was happening in the spiritual atmosphere and how it was affecting individuals. God had chosen to draw my attention to the people I loved, but it was never meant to end there. He entrusted me with this knowledge, not to keep it to myself but to respond, intercede, and see His beloved children walking in freedom. It was not a tool to shame or pass judgments but a gift from the Lord to see tangible change. The privilege to see through the eyes of a loving Father, to bring restoration, life, and ultimately God's redemptive purposes and strategies.

There have been so many experiences in my life like this one. Where out of the blue, I was consumed with feelings and thoughts flooding my mind and body. Countless occasions growing up—at family events, birthday celebrations, engagement parties, or weddings—where I had similar experiences. In a moment, I would experience abrupt changes to my mindset and lose my sense of myself. I wasn't thinking or acting the same; it was not who I was but I did not have an understanding that I was discerning others' emotions.

The spiritual realm was impacting those around me and would become all-consuming. If only I could have verbalized it, recognized that it was a gift. What if I had learned to distinguish my thoughts from the chatter in the spiritual atmosphere? What if I viewed it as a gift from God to feel what others felt, an insight into the thoughts of others? Not be overwhelmed or overcome by it but rather, in order to shift the atmosphere and see palpable change.

You see, people are bound by the enemy's schemes and have no idea that we are in a spiritual war. When we feel the pain, turmoil, heaviness, and bondage of others, there is the God of hope who came to set us free and we have the solution. God reveals it, because there's grace to heal it. The worthy Lamb that was slain, sets the captives free.

Activation: Discernment is a gift. Read through Hebrews 5:14 and reflect on your own journey. Allow the Holy Spirit to reveal His perspective.

Linger and Listen: What has the Holy Spirit revealed to you? Write it down.

Ask Jesus: Ask the Holy Spirit to reveal how the gift of discernment operates in your own life. Ask Jesus to reveal specific memories where you abruptly began feeling 'off' or not like your normal self, where you were in fact discerning the atmosphere.

Chapter 5

AWAKENING SENSITIVITY

I see my life in a very different way, knowing I have the gift of discernment.

A question I often ask myself now is, "Is this my normal?"

What Does Your Normal Look Like?

For me, the most important emphasis has been on becoming self-aware.

When I wake up, what emotions am I experiencing? How is my heart? When I am on my own, what do I think and feel? Whilst there are always opportunities for growth, inner healing, and re-writing neurological pathways, for the sake of this chapter, the focus is recognizing our own sphere of self in order to discern when we are picking up someone else's metron; to initiate and awaken sensitivity, becoming crucially self-aware. As we grow in self-awareness, we enter spaces, recognizing, almost immediately, when something does not feel right. I have learned to be conscious of my own thoughts, feelings, and responses. Once I am mindful of how I feel, what I think, and how my heart is at that moment, I can quickly identify when the environment around me has influenced my being. As I go about my day-today, I have my front foot forward, ready to respond at once when I know I am thinking out of character.

Walking through the grocery store, I brushed past a man and immediately felt a lack of peace; my heart raced. I felt rushed and agitated. The impulse to get out of that store as quickly as I could, pressed upon me. Although I could have brushed this off, I discerned that I had not felt this way seconds earlier. I picked up on how he was feeling as I watched him dart around the store, clearly in a panic to finish his shopping. This is an example of a daily interaction I have had. Having a lifetime of brief moments like these, I never thought twice about them. Moments in time where I have the authority to choose to make a significant difference in someone's life or ignore it. Just as he unintentionally released his anxiety, how much more can I purposefully release the Prince of Peace, life, hope, and joy? The presence of God has such a beautiful aroma. What a privilege to see tangible shifts in a person's life in a heartbeat by simply choosing to focus my attention and heart on the King of Kings.

I encourage you as you go about your daily life to leave your house intentionally, knowing how you are feeling and what your thoughts are for the day. In the interactions with others and the small moments in time, be aware of when you sense something outside of your normal reality. As you live each moment of the day, know that when you pick up on the emotions of others, you do not need to be overcome or overwhelmed by the atmosphere. As you discern things around you, you have the choice and the authority to respond to it, rather than succumb to it.

Don't Despise Small Beginnings

Begin with small, simple choices each day. Ask yourself, "What is my normal?"

Recognize when there is an immediate, dramatic change to your emotions, even subtle shifts. Being cognizant of this is so crucial in our walk with the Lord. We must be aware when we pick things up with our spiritual antennas, to be positioned to walk in authority and see those spiritual environments bow. We have more authority than we realize. This realization allows us to take action on behalf of those around us who are going through those particular emotions, to experience freedom.

Have you ever had a random thought come to mind of a friend or family member? I don't believe it is a coincidence but rather a nudge from the Holy Spirit to reach out to that individual or intercede on their behalf. I have found that when I reach out to them, they are often in need of something I can give them at that moment. Whether it's prayer, a prophetic word, revelation, an insight to share, or to remind them of a truth. I believe that this is also discerning, and as you walk in it, you awaken your spiritual sensitivity. God places an emotion, thought, or image in our minds in order to see the atmosphere move and for people to experience breakthroughs.

Always remember that greater is He who is in you than He who is in the world. The Holy Spirit lives in you; you are the light, and the Kingdom of God resides in you. Release love, joy, peace, all the fruits of the Spirit, and you will see the change that you are longing for. You will see those around you profoundly impacted and grateful. Discernment truly is a gift. Will you choose to use your gift to see atmospheres shift and lives changed? You have all that you need to do this.

I have given you many examples of how discernment has impacted my own life and the importance of where our attention and belief systems lie. Know that at any given moment, you can fix your gaze on Jesus; meditate on being in union with him, confident the Kingdom of God is in you, and to see His Kingdom come on earth as it is in Heaven! You carry the presence of God, as we are heirs of God and co-heirs with Christ, having the beautiful privilege of releasing the power of the Holy Spirit everywhere we walk.

Activation: Imagine yourself hidden under Jesus' wings. Take time to be still, give your heart space to feel. Draw in some deep breaths, quietening your body and mind. What are you feeling? What are you experiencing in your mind and body? What is your normal today? Tell Him.

Linger and Listen: Dream with God; see the Kingdom of God advance in your spheres of influence. What image, vision, or word has entered your heart from Him as you quiet yourself before Him?

Ask Jesus: As you spend time writing your grocery list, ask the Lord for people that you will encounter along the way. Know that everyone in that store longs to encounter the Prince of Peace. As you drive to the store, set your heart affection on the Lord, placing praise and thanksgiving on your lips. Not only will you notice the shift in the atmosphere, but you, too, will release that atmosphere into the store.

Chapter 6

MINDSET MATTERS

What if our heart's affection and where we focus our attention determines the atmosphere we create?

The mind directs our reality in every way: how we live, what we think, feel, say, and who we choose to interact with. We have been given authority and power to walk as He has called us to walk. Our mindsets are the driving force of our lives, controlling the lens through which we see the world and what we do and choose not to do. Mindsets liberate us, release freedom in our lives, or even hinder us, preventing us from walking in the fullness of who we've been called to be.

The way in which we experience our own lives is based on how we perceive the world in and around us. For example, there are two people who go through the exact same situation, but they recall the event from entirely different perspectives. Many times, I have assumed that what I experienced was similar to what others felt, yet that was not the case. If I chose to fix my thoughts on Jesus and the Kingdom of God, which is at hand, naturally, the fruit of peace, love, and joy would ruminate in every atmosphere I step into.

A mindset on the peace of God, the heart of God, and the love of Jesus would truly transform the atmosphere we release into the world. We become what we behold.

I recently heard Bill Johnson, Senior Leader of Bethel Church in Redding, California, share a testimony of being intentional in fixing his gaze on Jesus and turning his heart's affection towards God before entering a corner store. As he entered, the entire atmosphere of the store shifted and was filled with peace. The store owner told him that each time he came in, something changed in that place.

It is simply the principle of the Kingdom. If the Prince of Peace lives in us and we carry the Lord's peace then we can choose to release it as we walk. This may sound like we are mustering up the strength to produce peace, but this is far from what I am saying.

Behold: He Moves in Alignment with our Belief System and Faith

I have been pondering recently the significance of our belief systems. If I walk with the belief that I am loved, I will experience love; the same goes for me; if I believe no one likes me, then I will be rejected. Whatever we believe about ourselves is translated by the way we live and how people respond to us. If we believe that our presence will profoundly impact the lives around us, we become more aware of how we carry ourselves. If I believe I am a victim of the hardship and pain that I have experienced and felt, then I will remain a victim and be rendered powerless. Yet if I believe that God can and will set people free from life's chaos then I must know that I have the key to life and freedom which is only found in Jesus. Rather than seeing a victim as powerless, we get the privilege to use the key within us to set someone free. I long to grow in seeing the atmosphere shift around me as I partner with Heaven.

Steve Backland, Co-founder of Igniting Hope and Senior Associate Director of Bethel Leaders Network, states, "Any belief system that is not glistening with hope is rooted in a lie." So when our belief systems do not line up with how God sees us, there is a lie attached, and that requires repentance, forgiveness, and truth. To shatter the strongholds over your life or in order to walk others through freedom, you engage with the Holy Spirit. I ask Holy Spirit routinely to reveal any lies, the current state of my heart, and to show me the truth in the situation.

In studying past revivalists and the way they minister, I have observed that they were met with the amount of faith they possessed. Or rather, ministered uniquely with the beliefs that they had, confident in not just what they believed but what the Holy Spirit had revealed to them. God truly can move in any way He chooses and at any time, yet it blows my mind that He usually meets us at the level of faith we have at that moment and partners with us in every way. He often chooses a minister who has faith, believing God will show up. Let me clarify this statement. In watching a deliverance of demons, one preacher may say, "On the count of three, come out in Jesus' name – one, two, three." and the demon flees on three. Another may say, "Out now!" and it leaves immediately.

Countless times, I have watched or experienced God meeting each minister in a way they had faith to act upon and what they believed they should do. Whilst I acknowledge that it is not merely a matter of believing and it happens, but the revealing of the Holy Spirit. We can do nothing in and of ourselves; it is the power of the Holy Spirit at work through us. Yet as we read the Scriptures and, hear the testimonies and believe it for ourselves, in faith that comes from the Holy Spirit, everything changes.

What We Believe Matters

What we have faith for is made manifest in our lives. If we walk in authority with the belief system that the Lord desires to heal others through us, or that demons flee because the living God dwells within us, or that life is sustained through our hands, resurrection life is possible on every level here and now. The Holy Spirit has empowered us to demonstrate His love throughout the earth with signs, wonders, and miracles. When we walk in faith, confident that God will move, He shows up. It astounds me how the living God meets us in the measure of faith that we have.

Our faith is not in what we can do but rather in the One who lives in us. The belief systems have become the reality in which we live, rewiring neurological pathways and bringing us more in tune with the ways of God. I am convinced that it is His desire to use us in a greater measure of power than we've ever seen before. It is so crucial for us to align our minds and hearts with His. What we believe matters. It's time for the Bride to believe the truth of God's word and live full of faith, gaining a heavenly perspective over every circumstance in life.

Let the Spirit of Wisdom and the Spirit of Revelation reveal the truth and stir your faith. Get in the secret place with Jesus and ponder your belief systems. Are they aligned with what He believes?

I long for my belief systems to be determined by what God is saying and not merely by my earthly circumstances.

How does this become a reality?

Intimacy with the living God through His word, listening to His voice, deepening our understanding of His ways and His heart for humanity. To live with a mind conscious of the Lord, moving in step with the Spirit and living as the light He has called us to be. This is about us moving in step with the Holy Spirit. I am a new creation in Christ. I am His spotless Bride, I am chosen. Setting our mind on the things above, renewing and sanctifying it. This should be the focus as we walk hand in hand with the Lord.

Faith Moves Mountains

As my faith grows, I anticipate the Holy Spirit will move, atmospheres will shift, and lives will truly be changed. If we do not attach faith (without faith, it is impossible to please God), the impossible cannot be made possible. When we draw near to God, unrealistic viewpoints in nature immediately become realistic and achievable in our perspectives because it is no longer about us but about the God of the miraculous. As our faith increases, so do our belief systems. And as our belief systems shift, so do our actions, thoughts, words, and experiences. Everything is ever evolving, but to be transformed into the likeness of Christ, we must spend time with Christ to become like Him, as we prioritize Him, time with Him, beholding Him.

I love allowing God to speak through everything around me, especially out in nature, where I absolutely love to be. I'll choose something specific in the backyard as small as a blade of grass and ask, "God, what do you say about this?" or "God, who do you say I am?" And then I sing praises to Him, as He, too, in His loving kindness, sings His praise back to me. It is such a beautiful, intimate exchange. It takes time and practice to be still, to speak to Him, and to listen to the Spirit's gentle whispers as He speaks truths over your life and heart. He reminds you who you are and who He is.

Yes, being away and spending entire days with Him are the absolute dream. But, it is in the intimacy of the everyday moments-cleaning the dishes, showering, or running around the house getting things ready for the day that we can choose to enter a place of peace, stillness, and intimacy; he speaks, bringing life, love, and clarity.

"We cannot think like earth and expect heavenly results" —Bill Johnson.

This quote has profoundly impacted my life. In order to think like Heaven, we must spend time with the Maker of Heaven and Earth. We must prioritize time being still, growing in a heart of adoration, and attuned to His voice, His whisper. The one we love becomes the loudest voice. In a room full of hundreds of people, the voice of the one you love stands out more than all the others, following their voice. In the chaos, there is peace and clarity, and you know exactly where to turn and walk.

As we spend time with the one we love, all the noise and clatter are silenced. His voice becomes the clearest. He is wooing us into intimacy, a quiet place to be still before the one we love, allowing Him to take the heaviness we carry and restore our bodies, hearts, and minds back to a place of comfort and ultimate trust as we lean back in the loving arms of a beautiful Father. It is in these beautiful moments a divine exchange happens.

Words of Power

A few years ago, I was exploring Proverbs and the power of our tongue.

> *The tongue has the power of life and death, and those who love it will eat its fruit* (Proverbs 18:21 NIV).

A few friends and I were talking about the rice experiment conducted by Masaru Emoto. Dr Emoto spoke to three identical glass beakers of rice and water. In the first beaker he spoke kind, loving words; to the second, harsh words of death, and the third, silence; he simply ignored it. The one he spoke death to turned black; the one he ignored became moldy; but the one he spoke words of kindness and love to, fermented, producing life. A few friends and I decided to experiment further with plants. Speaking life to one plant and death to another. The one we spoke life to began to flourish but the one we spoke death to began to die.

If my words carry this much power upon plants, what impact do they have on myself and the people around me? What impact do my words have on my own body?

For over a decade, I had pimples on my face. I would often look at myself in the mirror and say, "I hate these pimples" and "You are ugly." If there was such power of life in my tongue maybe I could implement that in my own life.

One morning, I woke up and thought, *today I will begin to speak life over my face*. I began speaking to my face, "You are radiant, beautiful, and blemish-free. I love my face, and it radiates the glory of God." Within three days, I watched as every pimple vanished. My face began to radiate the glory of God! Friends were asking, "What happened? You look so different. You are glowing." This blew my mind. I spoke life and I received it. My face began to glow and look healthier and my countenance changed. Wow! How often have I spoken death over my body, over my strengths, weaknesses, characteristics, and even relationships. In all that we do we either sow death or life with the words we choose to speak.

What if we, as a body, unified, chose to speak life into every situation in our lives? What if we spoke life over our spouse, our friendships, our leaders, our colleagues, our churches. As we speak life, something so beautiful happens; life attracts life. The angelic are attracted to live; the heavenly hosts are attracted to live, and the presence of God is attracted to life; we usher in the Kingdom of God as we declare life. It brings unity to the body, healing, restoration, redemption, and understanding. We must be attentive to what we say because we release the very thing we speak.

Our faith, our belief systems, and what we speak are all entwined. It is out of the overflow of our heart that our mouth speaks.

A good man brings good things out of the good stored up in his heart, and an evil man brings evil things out of the evil stored up in his heart. For the mouth speaks what the heart is full of (Luke 6:45 NIV).

When we tune into what we are speaking, it is an indicator of what our heart is full of, of what we truly believe.

I want to be intimate with the words of life. Words that build up and not tear down. Words that bring life to a weary soul, bringing refreshment and rejuvenation. Speaking peace to anxiety releases a wave of peace that floods the mind and body. When we impart hope to the hopeless, there, hope is restored; when we speak of healing to the sick, there is healing. As we grow in our gift of discernment, feeling the array of emotions and thoughts, we are privileged to distribute life and see it touch the hearts of those around us.

Set Your Mind on What Matters

What we believe, what we declare, and how we partner with Heaven matters. We are living vessels set apart to do good works. We have authority and power and must recognize that we have been given the role to co-labor with the living God.

Let this be your prayer: I want to partner with you, God, to see Heaven come and lives restored. I want to see freedom for those bound and to disperse hopelessness, anxiety, and depression. I want to bring clarity to those living in chaos and confusion and see anxiety flee as the Prince of Peace enters in.

Holy Spirit, I call out for wisdom and understanding. Would you give me wisdom, the Spirit of Insight, and Revelation to reveal to me how I can partner with you to see you get your full reward. I want to know you, let your presence overwhelm me. Would you reveal areas in my life where I am not sowing life and would you teach me how to usher in the Kingdom of God and attract Heaven with my belief systems? Increase my awareness of the spheres of influence in my life.

Activation: In the beginning, we posed the question, "What if our heart's affection and where we focus our attention determines the atmosphere we create?" Take some time to recall where you focus your attention. Ask the Godhead to reveal how your thoughts are translated into your life. Your words carry power. Are there areas the Holy Spirit is revealing in which you have been speaking death, fear, doubt, hopelessness, or worry?

Linger and Listen: Take some time to be still and tell the Lord what you love about Him. Give Jesus your attention, your affection. Behold Him and be moved by God's heart.

Ask Jesus: God is the miracle-working God, ask Him to reveal His Heavenly perspective and declare life over every situation. Holy Spirit, can you reveal to me any areas in my life that I need to begin speaking life? Listen for His answer.

Chapter 7

TRUSTING THE REVEALER

The more I learn and grow, the more I realize how little I know, and the more I become aware of how completely dependent on the Holy Spirit I must be. He truly is the God of mysteries, and yet He chooses to reveal the mysteries of the Kingdom to us. I often ask in curiosity, "But why?" similar to a little child; other times I do not need to know, and all that is required of me is to simply trust. Trust in the Revealer, the all-knowing God; trust in Him to teach, enlighten, reveal, and equip me with all that I need. A life yielded to Him as I say, "yes" and watch Him teach me to use the gifts that He has given me.

As you are reading through these pages I sense some of you asking, "But why?" Why is it necessary for me to have the gift of discernment? Why me? It may feel more like a burden than a joy at times. I know for me, that was my reality.

Distinguishing Spirits was never meant to be a heavy burden for people to carry. It is a secret weapon, a weapon to release the peace of Heaven, the Kingdom of God, and the fruits of the Holy Spirit. Over the years, I have engaged in many conversations, hearing the heartbreak in which people thought they were going crazy and were treated accordingly. How many people are placed into psych wards or mental facilities for picking up spiritual atmospheres by seeing, feeling, and experiencing the spiritual climate that surrounds them? How many have thought something was off; choosing to remain at home, isolating from others, avoiding events or locations containing crowds? Many excused it as being "just introverts" and unable to cope around too many people. Maybe that is a reality for some. But what if they chose to avoid those environments that were divine set ups, for a very specific assignment, to shift the atmosphere in that place? What if you were meant to be the answer bringing the King of Kings with you?

It is often said that if you recognize a problem, you are the solution. What if the very area you are called to, that you have felt the need to avoid, is the very place you were meant to use your secret weapon? The gift is placed in your tool belt for His glory.

This is not a lesser gift; it is extraordinary!

It is so beautiful that the God of the Universe longs to partner with His children, that deeper connection, a heart set on the King, conversing with Him all day long, giving insight and His solutions to everyday situations.

Curiosity is a God Thing

Why, Daddy? Why, Mummy?" Parents delight in their children asking about the whys around them. They delight in the connection and curiosity. Curiosity is such a beautiful gift in the Kingdom. We must remain little children; we must remain curious.

God, help me to remain curious, to have an open heart, to ask without restriction. To come seeking to understand, for intimacy, for connection, for a heart that desires to grasp the ways of the

Kingdom. A heart waiting in anticipation for God to reveal insight into the Kingdom of God.

Secrets Treasured

I have emphasized that the Lord reveals information to us in order to intercede for others, but I also see His desire to speak to us and draw us into His heart. In humility, the Lord comes in so sweetly with a pure longing for connection and intimacy. In the gentle whispers, He reminds us of His desire and love for us to partner with Him.

When we discern what is occurring in the lives and the world around us, God reveals secrets to us, entrusting us with hidden mysteries. He is revealing this to us purely for connection, for intimacy. In the secrets, in the mystery, we are building history. He says, "My beloved, this information is just for you and Me." He divulges the hidden, and we treasure it in our heart. We build history with Him.

> *I will give you hidden treasures, riches stored in secret places, so that you may know that I am the LORD, the God of Israel, who summons you by name* (Isaiah 45:3 NIV).

As He reveals what is occurring in an atmosphere and the principalities over regions or what individuals are walking through, we are drawn deeper into His heart, being moved by His love and longing for His children to walk in fullness. He is revealing to us the keys for freedom for the Body of Christ, insights for the leaders, and wisdom from Heaven.

Gift, Not a Curse

I've come to realize that feeling an atmosphere has caused people a lot of pain, grief, isolation, confusion, and disappointment. It was never meant to be a curse, nor to cause pain or disillusionment. I have experienced this myself, feeling sick to my stomach with nausea, fear, or anxiety. I have felt completely disconnected from the Lord, as if blocked from hearing His voice or gaining revelation from the Word of God. At times, I have felt dizzy and instantly exhausted, as though I have been completely knocked out with horrible flu and need to sleep the days away. When we feel low, whether it is from our own environment or of others, the response of many is to retreat, work it out, and come back when there is a solution or clarity.

The path is lonely when we try to solve it. Some individuals with such a gift, disappear into their caves, going deeper into the feelings of what was seen, felt or experienced. How many are currently in their cave, wondering what they did wrong and how they got there? How many have asked themselves, "What more they can do to be sanctified?"

The Bible says we are washed as white as snow, and yet it feels like we are tainted with darkness and the realities of what the enemy is doing to steal, kill, and destroy. In my own experience, I have pushed friends, family and leaders away, trying to solve how and whys.

I am speaking to those who know their minds are renewed, who wake up to recognize the strange, abrupt change in thoughts, feelings, and mind, those images that are "not your normal."

The gift of discernment has consistently been misused.

I have experienced it in my own life and watched it in the lives of those around me. It was never intended to be misused but rather as an incredibly powerful weapon if used effectively by every child of God, a powerful weapon to obliterate the enemy's schemes over individual lives, cities, regions, and nations. We pray in the Lord's prayer, "Your Kingdom come on Earth as it is in Heaven," But we have a part to play for this to be a reality. God has given us responsibility and authority to be moved by His heart while simultaneously moving His heart. A child so intimate with the Father, with our head to His chest, we hear His heartbeat and are moved by the things He is moved by!

Imagine the army of God, confident in their authority to shift atmospheres, anchored in intimacy with Him, living life from Heaven, releasing God's Kingdom on earth!

Whatever we behold, we truly become. As Jesus lovers, beholding the Prince of Peace, peace is deeply embedded into every cell of our being. The atmosphere we enter into experiences the overflow.

I long to be so intimate with the Lord that I do not feel overwhelmed and burdened by fear, anxiety, depression, or the principalities that exist in a region.

As you talk to others and ponder this thought of why you have the gift of discernment, know that God has entrusted you with the gift to discern the spiritual atmosphere, the privilege of recognizing when people have been subject to the enemy's schemes, overcome by darkness. As God's children, carrying the indwelling presence of the Holy Spirit, we are co-laborers with Christ and influencing the spiritual climate around us with God's glorious light. It's time to ascend, to see what's happening in the Spiritual realm, and to live from our ascended position.

Activation: If you are feeling like you have been carrying this gift as a burden or other cares upon your shoulders, it's time to give those burdens to Jesus. As a prophetic act, brush your shoulders off, releasing anything that is stuck. Imagine Jesus above the cloud of darkness; hold your hands up and allow Jesus to take you by the hands to be raised with Christ.

Linger and Listen: Read Isaiah 45:3. Let Him reveal Himself to you as revelation is poured out.

Ask Jesus: What key to freedom do I carry in my hand? Why have you entrusted this gift to me?

Chapter 8

NAVIGATING VIVID IMAGES

Discerning the atmosphere through feeling and knowing can also include vivid images. This has happened to me often, and I know that I am not alone in this. I could write an entire book on the images I have seen with all the emotions, pain, and heartbreak accompanying them. I have experienced misunderstanding, confusion, and fear as all these images poured into my mind sporadically and spontaneously throughout my days. I imagine many of you reading this have had similar experiences.

For decades, I thought I was crazy, questioning whether there was something seriously wrong with me. What door had I opened to invite this into my life? Why was I seeing this? By watching a movie or listening to something, this entered in. It is true; we can open doors by who or what we expose ourselves to. However, there are times when we see what we see because we are discerning the spiritual environment. If we pick it up, chances are many other people around us will also feel the same way. We may see an image, and someone may come to mind at the next moment. That is not a coincidence.

I would often see images in my minds-eye. I have a creative mind and imagination, but these were unusual and threw me for a loop. Some things I saw were quite brutal. I feel it necessary here to share some of these images with you. I would be walking in a public space and see a picture of someone sitting alone, crying in a dark room, or someone in the throws of an anxiety attack. I saw multiple visions of suicide. Images of someone hanging themselves or dear friends lying lifeless on the ground in a pool of their own blood. It was horrible, graphic, and heart-wrenching all at once. I never really understood why these scenes would flash before my mind. I'd be walking the street, in a conversation with friends, sitting on a plane, or wherever I was, and these pictures would appear out of the blue. Many would pop into my mind as I traveled to different parts of the world in unfamiliar territory; images of women in slavery, in sex trafficking, children looking so fearful in dark barred rooms, rape, murder, gangs brutally attacking someone. Whilst they weren't anything I had physically seen or experienced, these scenes would taunt me for days, and I found myself feeling sick to my stomach. What was I meant to do? How should I respond? Who do I turn to? The images were always so vivid, as though I were there, watching on, as various emotions flooded my body, feelings of fear, panic, isolation, and abandonment.

Today, when I have an image, I ask the Lord how to pray, who to intercede on behalf of, and what it looks like to partner with Him in that situation. It could be for an individual or corporate setting, regional or the principalities over entire nations. Each time I receive an image, it is an opportunity to connect with the Lord, partner with Him, and intercede on behalf of the people He has entrusted me with, with hands opened and heart yielded to Him.

Each person's experience is unique and individual. You may see images or just know what is happening without feeling, hearing, or seeing anything. Then again, you may see traumatic visions of suicide, rape, or horrible sexual pictures, like I have, and feel shame or condemnation, not understanding fully their origin. If not aware, many see this believing that *they* are inherently wicked. If we are not careful, we can end up punishing ourselves with shame and condemnation, trying to fight it off, bewildered at what door we had opened to see such things, with confusion and uncertainty engulfing us. It creates a vicious cycle of questioning, leading us down a black hole we cannot escape.

Cry Out to Shift and Release

Once, I awoke in the middle of the night with an image of a woman and her son looking fearful in a field. She was plowing the ground as tears rolled down her face. The child working alongside her looked no older than three years old. I could see the fear and hopelessness so vivid in their eyes. I immediately knew the Holy Spirit had revealed to me that she had been trafficked and caught in slavery. I was filled with this passion, this righteous anger. I knew that I had to get out of bed and begin warring on their behalf. I got up, went to the garage, and began marching, praying, and crying out to the Lord for this beautiful family. Hours went by as I continued to intercede until I felt the shift. I sensed a release, and peace flooded my mind and body. There is power in prayer. We have authority, so when we intercede, something always happens. There is a shift when we cry out loud to Him.

I wish I had known then what I know now. I am still on this journey of discovery, learning, and growth, and I am asking all of the questions to the entrusted leaders and mentors I have been surrounded by.

As images come and go like the passing wind, I have a part to play, a role that is needed to partner with Heaven and intercede on behalf of the people He has entrusted me with. When I have vivid, brutal images, I now partner with the God of all hope and restoration. King Jesus died to save, heal, and deliver His people. It is a privilege to intercede—a joy. Only the God of Justice, the Spirit of Truth, is the One who can eradicate darkness by pouring out His marvelous light. Jesus is the answer, as Isaiah clearly lays out.

Is not this the kind of fasting I have chosen: to loose the chains of injustice and untie the cords of the yoke, to set the oppressed free and break every yoke? (Isaiah 58:6 NIV)

As we discern, our response will lose the chains of injustice and bring freedom and life. It does not end with seeing the image; it is the beginning of a beautiful partnership to see His Kingdom come into that situation.

For too long, I was consumed with disturbing images, tangled in shame and condemnation. Then I realized it is like having spiritual antennas, picking up the signal and tuning into the channel of what is happening around me. It could be in my close vicinity or a channel of what is happening on the other side of the world. Each experience requires an action and demands a response. In the past, when I felt condemnation, shame, and guilt, it drove me to hide.

What if sin was simply an area in the heart that had lost sight of its identity as a beloved child of the Creator of all? What if realignment was as simple as asking the Lord, "Who do you say that I am?"

Let that revelation sink in, both in mind and heart.

Activation: Isaiah 58:6–12 Holy Spirit, I thank you that you are the Spirit of Truth imparting insight, wisdom, and revelation to me each day. Create in me the heart that cries out for wisdom and calls aloud for understanding, searching it out. You are the solution, the answer to every problem. Would you increase my wisdom in how to partner with Heaven and release the Kingdom of God in my spheres of influence? What have you placed in my hand and entrusted me today?

Linger and Listen: Consider what stood out to you in this chapter. Listen to what God wants to reveal to you.

Ask Jesus: What does He want intercession to look like in your life? When an image comes to mind, ask God what the image means and who it is you get the privilege of interceding on behalf of. What action are you required to take? Are there memories you have of an image coming to mind, bringing confusion? Ask the Lord what He wants to say about what you saw.

Chapter 9

TOOLS FOR TRANSFORMATION

I recently went on a getaway to the coast, the most beautiful location by the ocean, with a dear friend of mine. Whilst vacations are a different pace of life, they often evoke various emotions for me. Here, I was filled with such peace, feeling refreshed and rejuvenated, inspired with a reignited vision. It brought new energy as I spent time dreaming of my future, a week my soul was craving as I recalibrated by the seaside.

When I returned home, it hit me like a ton of bricks. I tried rationalizing why I was exhausted: the 4 a.m. start, the early flight out of Burbank, Hollywood, and arriving home before 9 a.m.; it was valid to feel tired, yet as the day went on, all I wanted to do was lay on the couch, sleep, isolate myself from others, ignore calls and texts and binge watch Netflix. By the afternoon, I decided to journal to try to make sense of these emotions and the many thoughts of feeling hopeless about my future-feeling disappointed, apathetic, alone, and in deep despair.

I realized this level of hopelessness was not my normal. I could have dismissed it all, but as I spent time in the presence of God, He revealed to me that those thoughts and emotions present throughout the day were in fact, the gift of discernment as I was picking up on the atmosphere.

Are there times we may experience personal triggers from our past that we are to process? Absolutely! A smell, a sound, a memory, a statement, a vision, or even something that has caught a glimpse in the corner of our eyes. This can easily alter our feelings to seem 'out of the norm.' However, I believe it always comes back to self-awareness, tuning into the Holy Spirit, the truth in the Word of God, and input from trusted mentors, counselors, friends, and leaders in our lives.

So, as I journaled and re-read what I wrote, it felt somewhat strange to hear what I had written; it didn't sound like me or sit right in my spirit. Was this really what I was feeling? I felt confident it came from the atmosphere, so I tested it. I reached out to a few trusted peers who lived in the same area/atmosphere as me, people I knew who have a 'knowing' of what is in an atmosphere. I described what I was feeling. I was still very much stuck in the midst of the swirl and hopelessness, and everything in me wanted to remain in my 'cave' and sort it out on my own, but I knew I desperately needed the wisdom and counsel of trusted friends.

As I shared in detail what I was picking up and the feelings of the day, I asked, "Does any of this resonate with you? Have you experienced any of those same thoughts and feelings today?" All three responded immediately, confirming that they, too, were feeling exactly the same. They were also stuck in it, believing it was just a hard, hopeless day, but exposing what I noticed brought a realization that it was coming from the atmosphere and not themselves.

We were never meant to carry this alone or solve it on our own. We have the greatest weapon on Earth! The Lord God Almighty, the great Counselor, is speaking to us as the Body and revealing what is in the atmosphere, not to become burdened by it but to intercede and shift it. I see an army of the Lord's people rising up, unified in the spirit, walking hand in hand in deep fellowship. It is not about the lone ranger but the Body drawing strength from one another.

Practical Tools

One friend responded; "What do we do now?" We call it out: "Spirit of Hopelessness, I see you. I break any partnership I have made with you. I call on the God of Hope and release hope." We recognize what we are discerning and give it no authority in our lives. Once revealed, there is grace released to intercede on behalf of those who have partnered with the Spirit of Hopelessness.

I have found three steps invaluable on my journey to releasing the captives and redeeming the atmosphere.

1. Take Note and Press In

As mentioned in Chapter 5, as we assess ourselves and what our normal is, we will have greater clarity to recognize when we have discerned anything contrary to the Holy Spirit. You may just feel 'off.' It may be *a feeling in the body, a check or knowing in your spirit, seeing in the spirit realm, an abrupt picture in your mind, a whisper, or even a thought that comes to mind.* These are a few manifestations but not limited to the ways that you can discern the spiritual realm. It is the maturity to distinguish good and evil and specifically see where the enemy is present to steal, kill, and destroy.

When you sense this "spiritual disturbance," it is an invitation to press into the Lord for answers. We must walk in intimacy with

God, prioritizing the Word as our sustenance and wisdom. To recognize what's contrary to the Holy Spirit requires us to know the Spirit of Truth. If you don't yet know Him, meditate on the Word and invite the Holy Spirit to reveal who He is, to teach you His ways, and guide you in His truths.

2. Identify

What is it that you've discerned? We attune our ears to the Holy Spirit to engage in conversation with the All-Knowing God who extravagantly loves His children. *Identify what is impacting an individual or region, e.g. divination; witchcraft, control, manipulation, sexual impurity, rape, haughtiness; pride, arrogance, self-righteousness, fear, infirmity, deaf and dumb spirits, heaviness; hopelessness, anxiety, death, loneliness, greed, gluttony, idolatry, lying, deception, jealousy, disunity, chaos and confusion, etc.*

3. Call it Out and Release the Opposite

Declare, *"I see you, and I break all partnership with you and send you back to the pit. Now declare the opposite, that which is aligned with the fruits of the Holy Spirit."* In faith, we declare in confidence, knowing that God has chosen us as His dwelling place, a vessel entwined with the King of Glory.

On this journey of discerning, you will become more aware when someone is oppressed or has partnered with an evil spirit. I must emphasize it does not stop there. Do not go telling your friends all about what you think you may be picking up from someone. I have seen how destructive and heartbreaking it is when the Bride turns on one another and begins gossiping rather than taking the authority they have in Christ Jesus for freedom's sake. We stand on the belief that God is compelled by love, He is the deliverer, and in just one moment, God sets the captive free.

It is like the image of someone carrying a heavy bag that is weighing them down. As you approach them and say, "Let me take that from you. Jesus' yoke is easy, and His burden is light." It becomes our privilege to lead them to water, empowering them to fully submerge in the river of Living Water, where there is restoration. We are not to label a person by the spirit or, worse still, drive a person out of the community, but rather partner with the Lord to remove their burden, restore them with refreshing, and never judge them.

If it becomes clear that someone is oppressed by the demonic, stop; take communion, and declare the body and blood of the Lamb over them. Who the Son sets free is free indeed. We identify it and have the key to release freedom. Walking hand in hand to watch a glorious Bride unified.

> *However, do not rejoice that the spirits submit to you, but rejoice that your names are written in Heaven* (Luke 10:20 NIV).

It's less about identifying what the spirit is or casting it out and more about knowing that God's master plan is always to bring restoration to all creation. God is the deliverer, God is love and He sanctified us. We are not to fear darkness but rather, we must release His glorious light. It's time to get to work to see the Kingdom of God invade every life!

Clearing the Smoke

When I think of shifting atmospheres, I imagine what thick, dark smoke looks like when it has filled an area. Thoughts and feelings are heavy with despair and hopelessness and so depressing it makes the smoke darker and thicker. The smoke is suffocating and crippling individual lives until nothing else can be seen or experienced. The smoke doesn't belong, yet it lingers with the horrible stench of death. As we look to the One who is life and brings life abundantly, that which sows death, decay, and destruction must leave. I watch as He, the Bread of Life, the river of Living Water, flows into the environment; the strongholds of darkness, the demonic, and death dissipate like mist on a hot summer's day. His breath releases a glorious shimmer and the most wonderful fragrance.

Can you see it? Can you imagine it? The horrible black smoke leaves in an instant and is replaced with clear, delightfully refreshing air. Rather than darkness, the place is filled with light once again, the angelic flock as they join in with the chorus of Heaven; the Kingdom of God is here, and the place is flooded with an incense pleasing to the Lord, filled with love, hope, joy, and peace. In just a moment, one glimpse. We have been given all authority! Will we use that authority to obliterate darkness with His loving-kindness?

Breaking Agreements

Whilst meditating on Him and interceding causes the shift, there are also times when that does not work and will not work. Every situation is different and requires wisdom and insight. When people choose to partner and make legal agreements (contracts) with the enemy, these are strongholds over them and they are bound by chains. This can happen when lies are believed, or there is any unforgiveness, fear, hatred, sexual sin, or occult practices such as witchcraft. We make agreements based on the belief systems we have, the actions we take, and what we have come into agreement with within our thoughts about ourselves and others.

I recall a time when the moment I entered a church building for a Sunday morning service, I felt worthless; even thinking suicidal thoughts, my mind plotted how to kill myself. These dark, twisted thoughts were not there just minutes ago. I stood worshiping Jesus, my favorite thing to do, but my mind was a dark cloud. The pain of depression was so intense, as though a weighted blanket of darkness was placed on top of my head, holding me down. I had walked in discernment long enough to know that I was picking up what was in the atmosphere, so I did what I always did. I asked the Holy Spirit, "Would you reveal to me who I am picking this up from? Who has partnered with the Spirit of Suicide?" In the Lord's kindness, my attention was immediately drawn to the man at the end of the row directly in front of me. The Holy Spirit revealed who he was and that he was struggling with depression and suicidal thoughts. I knew I had the privilege of interceding, so in worship, as I looked to King Jesus, I began interceding on behalf of this beloved child of God.

Nothing happened.

I was shocked and couldn't understand why my thought life was still a dark swirl under the weight of depression. It felt personal. I thought *maybe I am the one who is depressed and needed to end my life*. I began to imagine the different ways that I would accomplish this. It is never a good idea to come under the weight of the environment; we must brush it off and call out what we see. I declared, "Spirit of Suicide, I see you and break any partnership I have made with you. I call on the God of life and hope and release abundant life." I would like to tell you that it left, and I felt peace and joy again, but it did not shift, and all I kept thinking about was how I should end my life. Hours later, I left the building as it continued to linger on my mind like black ink. I shared this with a friend who was with me; what I had discerned but couldn't shift, so she prayed over me, brushing any remnants off. It left just as quickly as it came. This experience was new to me, and I was determined to discover what happened.

Through conversations with trusted friends and leaders, I learned that this man had opened the door to hatred and had partnered with the Spirit of Suicide. He had agreed with thoughts of self-hatred. So, what would I have done differently? When speaking to Dawna DeSilva, founder of Bethel Sozo, her first question was, "Did you engage the person?" My response was, "Well, no." It seems obvious in hindsight. Dawna explained, "Often it is the enemy who wants to harass the person, and it's not until you engage the person in conversation and begin to speak life, is life released. Once you call it out, it tries to hide; it wants to flee but doesn't want to be noticed. There is a difference whether the attack is coming *at* a person or coming *from* them."

When we make partnerships with the enemy, saying, "I am not worthy of love," "I will never be loved," or "My life is worthless," we form an agreement or contract with these lies.

To know what to do, you must converse with the person to gain understanding of what they are thinking and feeling. You must obtain permission to speak the opposite of what you have discerned in the atmosphere. If something is coming *from* someone, there is a need for them to break agreements through repentance and forgiveness. In the example of my experience at church, I needed to talk with the man and find out how he was doing. I needed to declare out loud to expose the enemy's lies and for the man to hear the Kingdom truth that his life was valuable and long to see him set free. It could be as simple as stating: "You are loved, and your life is valuable". My heart and longing is always to see people set free, and the beauty of freedom is that it is always a choice.

Are you feeling what is in the atmosphere? Be still before God and ask questions. If He reveals someone is oppressed, begin by interceding, praying, and shifting. If it doesn't shift, it is likely that agreements have been made. Engage the person in conversation for keys that you may identify. Perhaps you are not picking up on an individual but rather a corporate situation.

Your response will be different and determined by the role you have in the environment you are in. If you are in leadership, engage other leaders in conversation, see if they are discerning the same thing, and determine corporately what steps to take next. Be aware of your role in that location and if you have been given authority to share. Whilst the practical responses may differ slightly, walk in confidence that *"the one who is in you is greater than the one who is in the world"* (1 John 4:4 NIV). In the example I shared, when I returned home from my trip, I was at home alone, discerning the atmosphere of the region. I contacted trusted friends and recognized we were all discerning the same thing, so I stopped, worshiped, and prayed until I personally felt a shift. It is not a "one size fits all" solution every time.

We must be serious about taking our thoughts captive. Lies enter as thoughts.

We demolish arguments and every pretension that sets itself up against the knowledge of God, and we take captive every thought to make it obedient to Christ (2 Corinthians 10:5 NIV).

When we make our thoughts obedient to Christ, those strongholds dissipate. We have a Savior who died for His children to be saved, healed, and delivered. The blood of Jesus cleanses us from all sin and shame. Discernment is a beautiful gift, but we must align our thoughts with His thoughts about us. We must walk in freedom to lead others into freedom.

Activation: Sit down with the Lord and explore what thought comes to mind as you read this statement; "If they knew this thing about me, then I would never be loved". Firstly, sit vulnerably before your loving Saviour, take that backpack off, and give it to Jesus. Then, choose someone trusted and safe to be vulnerable with and share this thought.

Linger and Listen: We each have unique gifting, personalities. Let God reveal to you what tools/strategies He has entrusted to you.

Ask Jesus: Picture yourself or someone carrying a heavy backpack. Ask the Holy Spirit, how do I partner with you to release your beloved child from that weight? Are there repeated patterns of thoughts that I have which have built strongholds in my own life?

Chapter 10

COMMUNITY

As we run after the Lord together, we must become comfortable with allowing others to speak into our lives. Our hearts must be open and malleable, willing for the Holy Spirit to reveal truth to us, as well as through the people around us. Invite friends and family into your journey and give them permission to call out when you have taken on or are carrying false responsibility for what you have discerned. I have learned over the years that we have been created to journey *in* community and *with* community.

Many times, I have chosen to isolate, opting for independence while overwhelmed and weighed down by the atmosphere. I have watched as many, like myself, were determined they must work it out, solve it alone, and step into freedom before they can resurface from their secret place and call it Holy. This is often disguised as a time of holiness when it is really just escaping those around us because we are on a mission to solve our problems or what we are discerning on our own. It is destructive and isolating and causes us to move away from being unified in a community.

I have noticed a pattern when 'feelers' crawl into their cave under the weight and shame rather than invite their community in and brush it off. What if that was never God's design? I long for and need community in my life and have learned to truly lean on those around me.

Now, each time I feel 'off' and instantly want to run away, I choose to run into the arms of the community to seek counsel from trusted friends, family, and leaders. I have discovered there are those who also feel what is in an atmosphere, and I have chosen to confide in them. I describe what I have felt, seen, and experienced to them, and like a breath of relief, they realize they, too, have been feeling the same thing, struggling alone to work out what was wrong with them.

Light and Truth

It is not a coincidence that many discerning people feel the same way. In fact, it sheds light on what is happening in the atmosphere. If a few gather and all pick up the same thing, then there is a fair chance that there is more than just a few of you, and it is an army of people experiencing the same thing at the same time. With that insight, it sheds light on what to do and how to respond. Within community, we are reminded of who we are; we recalibrate and recognize that, once again, it is in the atmosphere. It is in the power of community to lead us into greater freedom. In community, we intercede on behalf of the region, with one another, unified in one Spirit, the Holy Spirit, to release the Kingdom of life, light, and truth.

Community isn't just a nice add-on to our lives; it is as crucial as breathing. For too long, we have tried to convince ourselves that independence is the way forward. It has to change; we must shift our belief systems and value community as of utmost importance. In fact, being a community is so significant that studies have shown that when babies are left in isolation with no human interaction, no touch or affection, they will lose weight and eventually die. Human isolation is a form of torture, breeding insanity. Western culture fights for independence. We wear it like a badge of honor and proclaim that it is the best way to live. When pursuing independence solely, we do not allow anyone into what we are feeling. We have no reason to be vulnerable or to invite others into our journey. I highlight independence because, in my season of growing in the gift of discernment, I have come to learn that thriving is not possible in isolation.

Coming face-to-face with familiar spirits and discerning what is coming from the atmosphere around us or from us is not something we were meant to do on our own. It requires wisdom and prayer warriors. It is an everyday journey of walking with Him, of pursuing His voice, of pursuing Him together. Yes, God, the great revealer, has also revealed a mystery to us—the Church—The Body of Christ, placing a divine emphasis on unity, community, and fellowship. There are many days I must turn to trusted friends, cherishing their wisdom. I require their input to test what I am experiencing in a like-minded community of on-fire believers who are pursuing the Word and His voice in each moment.

Often, when we don't feel like we are ourselves, we become introspective. We analyze why we are not ok and walk through every scenario that has happened in the days before. What led me to feel this? What door did I open? What did I expose myself to? In the questioning, I found, for me, this came from a place of anxiety and performance. The mentality of, 'Well, I got myself into this mess, and I am the only one who can get myself out of it.' A mindset believing that I have to work it out on my own. This leads to inner turmoil and a downward spiral. The more I think and try to solve all that is coming up, the more I desire to isolate myself from others. Now, this is not to negate the need for inner healing or even counseling. I have a high value for counseling and pursuing inner healing in every way, for they are not only necessary but crucial for our health. In fact, we must know our identity as a child of God and receive freedom in order to discern with clarity.

Within our gift of discerning the atmosphere around us, I wonder how many people isolate themselves from everyone and go into their cave as they are tossed by the waves they feel, swept into a tornado of unfamiliar thoughts and emotions. This is when we must turn towards our community most. This is when we must express what we are feeling, receiving trusted wisdom and counsel from those around us.

Agreement

There is something so beautiful when you gather to intercede and pursue the Lord together. Like a sparkler being ignited, you could burn one alone or choose to light the entire packet at once. The ignition, fire, and heat are significantly greater as sparklers gather together in close proximity.

I am reminded of the verse in Matthew:

> *Again, truly I tell you that if two of you on Earth agree about anything they ask for, it will be done for them by my Father in Heaven. For where two or three gather in my name, there I am with them* (Matthew 18:19–20 ESV).

This is a huge statement. The weight of the significance of two or three gathering in the name of Jesus. The magnitude of being unified in the spirit and in fellowship as we come before our Father in Heaven and God responds. "There I am" he says. His presence is with us, and anything asked for will be done. We gather within our community with intentionality. What a privilege it is to be entrusted to ask in alignment with God's heart, and it will be done. We feel the pleasure of Jesus as we gather and ask of Him. The Kingdom of God only functions in community and fellowship, as demonstrated by the Trinity first and foremost. The Father responds and is moved when we gather together and pray. In the name of Jesus, we gather; in the name of Jesus, we agree; in the name of Jesus, we ask. Jesus gathers with us, the omnipresent King responding to us.

In community, we share what we are discerning, recognizing what has felt "off", and we decree the opposite in the name of Jesus. We have a part to play in shifting the atmosphere and seeing darkness obliterated. We have a role to play when we discern what is happening in our sphere of influence. It is a significant role. If everyone lived heaven-conscious and focused on seeing the Kingdom of Heaven infiltrated into every area of our sphere of influence, everything would change. It takes people to align, unite, gather, and lead one another to point to Him.

I liken it to a group of people gathered together in the evening. All of a sudden, one person, a leader, a pioneer, points upwards towards the sky. A shooting star is seen before their eyes. It just takes one person to draw attention towards the star for all to see it.

This vision of pointing to a shooting star is a picture of the gift of discernment. It is a recognition of what is happening in the atmosphere in the moment, directing your gaze to how He is moving and what He is doing in it. As the body of Christ collectively discerns the spiritual atmosphere, it brings clarity and shifts perspectives. This brings fresh revelation to all, to see the miraculous work that God is doing, revealing light in the darkness, beholding the glory of God. Inviting our community into those moments when you have chosen isolation. Point and recalibrate in order to see Him clearly, to see Him rightly, and to recognize from Heaven's perspective all that is happening around you and in you. Rend the heavens and see Heaven invade Earth.

Activation: Pursue connection with those people and develop a community of like-minded individuals you can share what you are feeling, and hone in on what you are discerning, whether it is your own, the immediate environment you are in (such as home, church, shops, park), the region or the nation, etc.

Linger and Listen: Pause and ask the Holy Spirit to reveal trusted leaders and friends in your environment with the gift of discernment.

Ask Jesus: Ask the Holy Spirit who it is that you can connect with and test what you are feeling. It must be someone rooted in intimacy with the Lord.

Chapter 11

LEADERSHIP

We are not only meant to discern what is happening in the atmosphere but to highlight what is on the Lord's heart, to recognize what He is doing, and to receive strategies to partner with Christ and see a shift. Our gaze fixed on Jesus, hearing Abba Father's heartbeat for His children. When you share with your own community what you are discerning in a given moment, you point to what He is doing for the benefit of those around you. If you are discerning anxiety, He is releasing peace, if you are sensing oppression, He is setting the captive free, if you are feeling lonely, He is gathering and unifying the body. If you are seeing inappropriate sexual images, He is releasing purity. As we feel the pain and heartbreak, we are empowered to release the opposite.

Choose to be attentive to any shifts you recognize in your personal mindsets or emotions as you enter into fellowship with your community. Allow yourself time to sit with the Holy Spirit and realize what you are perceiving within your church congregation. Ask for the Spirit of Wisdom and Understanding in discernment. As God reveals it, choose to invite your trusted people in and ask them what they are perceiving at that moment or throughout the week. Choose vulnerability. It's ok to be wrong as we must consistently 'test' and seek counsel on this journey.

It is God's delight to give us keys to discern and wisdom to unlock hearts and minds. What we pick up is simply a clue entrusted to us, to intercede and see the Kingdom of God advance in our spheres of influence.

Will You Say Yes?

God is always working, always revealing, and always looking for willing vessels who say, "Yes, use me. Reveal how you are moving and give me wisdom on how I can partner with you to release your strategies on Earth." He is a strategic God. He is always good. He gives good gifts to His children, and then He teaches us how to use them. It is not an accident or a coincidence that He has personally chosen you with the gift of discernment. He has fully equipped you! He has given you all the artillery needed to partner with Heaven.

Will you say yes?

We are required to respond to what we are discerning, whether it is a feeling in the body, a knowing or seeing. We must establish partnerships with trusted leaders. We need a team of intercessors who are tapping into what is occurring. Imagine a congregation that is locked on to God's heartbeat, what he is doing, and how He is moving. A team constantly shedding light on what is perceived, with intercessors releasing the opposite. A congregation in connection with Heavenly strategies. Partnering with Him to see freedom and life abundant.

I am reminded of Solomon. He had a dream, and in his dream, he asked for discernment to govern the people. This pleased the Lord.

"So give your servant a discerning heart to govern your people and to distinguish between right and wrong. For who is able to govern this great people of yours?" The Lord was pleased that Solomon had asked for this. So God said to him,

> *Since you have asked for this and not for long life or wealth for yourself, nor have asked for the death of your enemies but for discernment in administering justice, I will do what you have asked* (1 Kings 3:9–12 NIV).

Solomon requested a discerning heart to govern the people. Whilst this was a dream, I believe it is important for leaders to have discernment and to utilize it as a gift to lead with wisdom. It is significant and necessary to share what we perceive with leadership, mentors, and those trusted few around us. This gift is not to be used in isolation, alone in our prayer closet. This is a gift needed for our community, our spheres of influence, and for those we love. If you haven't already, it is time to gather people in your community that God has highlighted. Prioritize meeting together and sharing.

We have a leadership role to think beyond ourselves, focused on His Kingdom invading Earth through our spheres of influence. A role that will profoundly touch and impact those around us if we choose to say yes, to press in, and to see the change we are longing for. It is time to see the shift we have dreamt of and to see a body of believers, walking in freedom, in fullness, with their gaze fixed upward, solely on Him.

As we discern, as we gather, and as we invite leadership to participate, they, too, will gain wisdom in how to respond and lead the congregation with momentum. And as we partner with the momentum of what our Savior is doing through us, we will see exponential growth and change.

This gift is extraordinary, but in humility and love, it must move forward. Discernment is a gift from the Holy Spirit to see His liquid love invade lives. Let's build trust and rapport with our leaders and community. Discernment is not greater than other gifts; for all are needed and necessary. Our posture must always be to serve, intentionally honoring our leaders and those around us. Honor is tangible; show it by voicing the impact those in leadership have had on you. And if your leaders do not yet recognize the value of the gifts of the Holy Spirit in the body of Christ, you have the privilege of stewarding it with a few trusted people. It takes but two or three to gather, press in, and intercede in love and humility. It is a journey for everyone. The dream is for the body to be attuned to the voice of God and His heartbeat.

Activation: Seek revelation as you read 1 Kings 3:7–15.

Linger and Listen: Receive the strategies released to you from Heaven. It will look unique in your own community.

Ask Jesus: How can I partner with you to use the gift of discernment for your glory? Would you reveal to me what my role is in this season? Holy Spirit, you know my community, my church. Would you reveal to me your wisdom in the steps I need to take moving forward? Remember: humility is the way forward.

Chapter 12

FLOW IN THE GIFT

I have come to realize that I always have to be 'on.' It is a never-ending journey. It would be so nice to 'arrive' at a destination – all sorted, solved, and submitted, like completing an assignment. Rather, it is a daily journey, like waves rolling in and out to sea. Watching the current as it ebbs and flows, pulling the water back as it is displaced in preparation for the larger set of waves that will soon appear on the horizon. It is the ebb and flow, the highs and lows, the joys and the triumphs, the pain, and the confusion; it's the existence of the spiritual realm intermingled with our beautiful thought-life, emotions, belief systems, and interactions. It requires constant attention as we navigate all that we feel and discern.

I have often blamed the 'pain' that I was feeling as an atmospheric thing and this can be destructive. We must give space for our hearts to explore what is evoked in a moment. Feelings simmering to the surface require attention. Being the healthiest version of ourselves demands us to be present within our hearts and thoughts. It is important to not palm off the pains, the triggers that rise to the top, but rather, process them.

Self-Awareness

The gift of discernment is not something that ends and then you part ways, but instead flows in. When the weight of the atmosphere becomes too much, don't let it cling to you. Recalibrate, brush it off, and receive a fresh perspective. Some experiencing this gift do all that they can to avoid emotions associated with pain and disappointment. They cope by numbing their feelings entirely and detaching from their heart. To remain healthy, press in further to discernment into your heart responses. As we listen to our hearts and grow in self-awareness, we will learn to take ownership of what is truly our personal feelings. Self-awareness brings clarity to the gift of discernment. When our feelings are stirred, we can know what our normal is and recognize when our heart needs space to process or when we've picked up the feelings in the atmosphere. It becomes blatantly apparent that each requires different responses. Our equilibrium comes from listening attentively to our heart, mind, and body and, most importantly, the great revealer of truth, the Holy Spirit.

My mentor once said, "You're giving the devil too much credit." I grew up believing that any emotion outside of happiness was evil; it was the enemy out to get me. This left me building walls as thick as concrete around my heart, locked in tight by a steel vault. Nothing could get in and nothing could get out. I had chosen to suppress all emotions to the point of numbness. I was afraid of what I felt and the impact it might have on me and those around me. I never wanted to expose my greatest fears and insecurities to anyone.

This journey of discovery has been good for me. I learned to take time to own what feelings truly were mine. I invited trusted leaders, friends, and family into my fears, darkest thoughts, and frailties, allowing them to see me and love me through it. I found that I needed those I deeply trusted, with whom I could externally process my thoughts and emotions, those who could counsel me or lead me through a Sozo for personal deliverance.

Chosen, Beloved

Jesus paid the ultimate price for us to be saved, healed, and delivered. Yet so many are still living in bondage with the mentality of being a slave of God. Jesus longs for us to become children of God, to break off the orphan spirit, and to live in authority where we have been adopted into Sonship. It is time for God's chosen, beloved children, to live in the reality and have full access to the freedom that Jesus has made available to us. Yes, Jesus has paid the ultimate price, but it requires something of us – it requires us to receive the gift by grace through faith. To break off lies and mindsets of the flesh and embrace the realities of the truths of the gospel. It is vital for us to turn to the Holy Spirit and allow Him to reveal what is coming up in our hearts and to help us become self-aware of any limiting, disbelieving, mindsets that are holding us captive and in bondage.

It is in self-awareness and giving the heart permission to feel, the fortress of stone crumbles, and vulnerably allows love in. The road for me often felt so stressful, messy, uncomfortable and clunky as neurological pathways were rewritten and healthier responses to triggers, were established. As I took ownership of my emotions and pursued inner healing, the atmospheres that I discerned no longer felt overwhelming and chaotic but rather as insight from Heaven.

Honestly, there are times I wish I could switch off discernment like a lightbulb. Or it was perhaps like a traffic signal indicating whether what I was experiencing was on my own or in the atmosphere. Self-awareness is a key to regulation.

As my self-awareness grew, I recognized that many battles I fought to shift the atmosphere were truly my own pains bubbling to the surface. How many hours have I spent warring on behalf of others when all I truly needed was my loving Abba Father to hold me against His chest and embrace me as I wept? And to be lovingly supported by a community that enables vulnerability, prioritizes connection, and values God's presence in the pain. I am done carrying this alone. Community has more than shown me this. Seek those who, by experience, have walked this road, learned to be self-aware, and are pursuing inner healing.

As you grow in self-awareness and give space for your heart to feel and process, I believe your wisdom will grow, and discerning will bring clarity instead of confusion.

Activation: God, I thank you for my heart and the gift of allowing my heart space to feel.

Ask: Heart, what do you need? Heart, are there areas I have neglected you? Holy Spirit, increase my wisdom to discern when these feelings are my own and when I am discerning the atmosphere.

Linger and Listen: The heart, mind, and spirit are all entwined. There are times we give one too much attention. There are times we must say, "Heart and the mind be silent, and in the name of Jesus, I command the spirit to come forward."

Ask Jesus: Have I neglected my heart, mind, or spirit? Sit with Jesus; what does He want to say to you about your heart?

Chapter 13

SHIFTING

Let's begin dreaming with God to see the impossible made possible. Let's partner with Him to see mankind restored and experience freedom, breakthrough, and life in abundance. God is the miracle worker. Where the presence of the Lord is, there are signs, wonders, and miracles. Jesus performed many miracles and impacted the world around Him in every way. We have been given the authority to co-labor and co-create with Him. We are God's vessels, and He loves to partner with us.

Testimonies Through Declarations of Faith

Faith is stirred as we hear what God has done in and through us.

As I was in a Zoom class one day, I heard one testimony after the next of co-laborering with Christ. The teacher recounted a time when visiting a beach and partnering with God, the weather was shifted. My heart was stirred as I listened. I decided to further discover this reality for myself.

As I sat down under the pergola of my beautiful home in Sydney, Australia, continuing to listen to these stories, the clouds grew black, and it began pouring rain. If God had done it before, He can absolutely do it again. We know faith as small as a mustard seed can move mountains. The class had finished, and my friend and I looked at each other with sweet excitement and anticipation. We declared that the rain would stop and the sun would come out between the times 1:30 pm and 3 pm. Thirty minutes later, we witnessed the clouds part like a curtain, opening wide to reveal a bright blue, cloud-free sky within seconds. The rain immediately stopped, and the grass, which only moments ago was completely drenched by the pouring rain, dried up before our very eyes. As three p.m. hit, the black clouds reappeared out of nowhere and immediately rolled across the sky quicker than I had ever seen, filling the sky above once again with the blackened, eerie feeling of a looming storm.

Just a week later, a dear friend of mine was celebrating a birthday. Her desire for her birthday was to have a picnic with a charcuterie board on the cliff face overlooking the ocean. However, once again, it was pouring down with rain. Our friend had asked us several times, "It is raining, so what is our plan B?" But we had insisted that there was no plan B, and declared that the clouds would part to reveal blue sky and the rain would cease. We had seen it only a week earlier, so we were full of faith that we would see it again. As we drove towards the ocean, the rain fell in buckets, but we kept on driving, declaring in faith that the rain would subside in seventeen minutes. We drove towards the ocean with the windscreen wipers at the highest speed. As we pulled up to park the car, just walking distance from the lookout, the rain immediately stopped. Literally, the moment we parked, the rain ceased! We walked along the cliff face to the desired spot for a birthday lookout and were in awe of God that the rain had subsided entirely. We had our picnic, watching in wonder of the God of the Universe working on our behalf; the clouds moved rapidly across the sky, parting ways for the sun to come out and the blue sky to appear above us. With grateful hearts and thankfulness, I was once again moved by how loving and intentional God is. He cares so deeply for His children and their desires. It felt like a kiss from Heaven as we celebrated.

We have the authority to shift the weather. We have the authority to co-labor with Jesus as we are in union with Him and adopted as children of the living God.

Faith Upon Faith

One sunny afternoon, I was spending time with my brother, enjoying the Australian coastline on one of my favorite beaches. As we sat on the white sand, I heard a rumbling rising up from behind the mountains. Thick black clouds headed directly towards us. It was one of those storms that appeared literally out of nowhere. The sky in the distance turned black with rumblings of thunder, flashes of lightning in the clouds, and a strong gust of wind. It was a spectacular sight. I watched as everyone on the beach abruptly grabbed their beach things and ran towards their cars, knowing it would be only minutes before they were absolutely saturated by the looming downpour of quite a violent storm. I remained seated on my beach towel, watching the scene play out as panicked families dashed about and the thunder grew louder and louder. At that moment, I recalled the previous two times when the weather had shifted as I had partnered with the Lord. In my response to the remembrance of what God had done before,

I commanded the clouds to alter direction, go around us, move south, and for the storm to head towards the ocean. We sat and watched as the clouds shifted immediately. I was confident that we did not need to leave. The clouds heading directly east shifted and moved around us, around the beach, and out toward the sea on the horizon. The storm did not touch us on the sand but moved southeast of us into the ocean. The clouds remained black, and the thunder and lightning continued the entire time, yet it did not touch us. It felt like another kiss from Heaven. Then, after all that, the most beautiful rainbow appeared in the clouds. It was quite the phenomenon.

Oh, His loving kindness! I felt the pleasure of God and His love wash over me.

A few months later I was in Redding, California, with a dear friend of mine, walking along a path, sharing testimonies of being co-heirs with Christ. I told her my accumulated testimonies of shifting the weather and of the authority we have been given in Jesus' name. It was particularly windy that day. Time to put it into practice – so I told her to declare, "Wind be still." As she did, the breeze slowed to a stop around us. We observed the trees all swaying around us from the wind, but there was absolutely no breeze on us! It was for a short time, then the wind picked back up again. But in that brief moment, she looked at me in complete shock at what was happening. This was another moment of partnering with Him and the beautiful demonstration of God's sheer Power at work in and through His children's hands.

As Small as a Mustard Seed

One thing I know is that faith as small as a mustard seed can move mountains. I walk in faith, knowing that it is Jesus living in me that makes all possible. Faith seeps into every area of my life. Faith enables a believer to walk in the fullness of Christ. It is in faith that we see the unraveling of the impossible made possible. Like the authority to shift weather, we have authority in the atmosphere around us. Just as the clouds part, the sun, and the blue sky appear, and we get the privilege of partnering with Jesus and shifting the darkened clouds over someone's life to dissipate in the name of Jesus. The black clouds lift, and the brain fog, confusion, depression, anxiety, and hopelessness are replaced with the realities of the Kingdom of Heaven: love, joy, peace, and patience. It is such a beautiful gift that the Father has given us to intercede on behalf of those who are submerged in darkness. We owe the world around us an encounter with the Living God.

All creation in Heaven and Earth cries out in praise to bring glory to the King of Kings.

> *On the day the LORD gave the Amorites over to Israel, Joshua said to the LORD in the presence of Israel: "Sun, stand still over Gibeon, and you, moon, over the Valley of Aijalon. So the sun stood still, and the moon stopped, till the nation avenged itself on its enemies, as it is written in the Book of Jashar. The sun stopped in the middle of the sky and delayed going down about a full day"* (Joshua 10:12-13 NIV).

Joshua declared that the sun and moon would stand still, and they did. They stopped. As Joshua spoke, it happened; the atmosphere shifted. In the physical natural realm, the sun and the moon held their positions and did not move.

Elijah was a man of faith. There was a severe drought across the land and Elijah had faith to believe the rain was coming.

Elijah, Jesus and You

> *"Go and look toward the sea," he told his servant. And he went up and looked. "There is nothing there," he said. Seven times Elijah said, "Go back." The seventh time the servant reported, "A cloud as small as a man's hand is rising from the sea." So Elijah said, "Go and tell Ahab, 'Hitch up your chariot and go down before the rain stops you.'" Meanwhile, the sky grew black with clouds, the wind rose, heavy rain started falling and Ahab rode off to Jezreel. The power of the Lord came on Elijah and, tucking his cloak into his belt, he ran ahead of Ahab all the way to Jezreel* (1 Kings 18:43–48 NIV).

Then of course there was Jesus at the Sea of Galilee commanding that the wind and the waves be still.

> *He got up, rebuked the wind and said to the waves, "Quiet! Be still!" Then the wind died down and it was completely calm. He said to his disciples, "Why are you so afraid? Do you still have no faith?" They were terrified and asked each other, "Who is this? Even the wind and the waves obey him!"* (Mark 4: 39-41 NIV).

This is such a profound story. The disciples were terrified, full of fear as they saw the wind and the waves. Yet Jesus was sound asleep. His focus was not on the darkness and what was happening around Him. He operated in the glory realm, seeing things from a Heavenly perspective. If Jesus is my example and I am called to live like Christ, I am also given the authority to do what He did. In fact, it says that we will do even greater works than He. Wow! How could we do greater works than Him?

All things in Heaven and Earth have been subject to us.

I grew up where there were many birds flying and chirping around our home. When I moved, I noticed it was completely quiet outside all day long. I missed the sound of birds chirping; they are reminders for me of the Lord singing over me. I was talking to the Lord and telling Him my desire for the music of birds to resound around my home. So I called the birds to begin singing. Out of the trees in the distance, birds that had been silent for months on end immediately began to sing. They flew near and even sat in the trees around me, singing such beautiful melodies. The happy chatter of the birds was like beautiful incense to the Lord. Day in and day out, all sorts of birds sang out. It became so common that even at 1 am in the morning, birds were chirping. On several occasions, my housemate would request that I ask the birds to stop singing so that she could sleep, and of course, they would then be silent overnight until the following day, when they would start up again.

For the creation waits in eager expectation for the children of God to be revealed (Romans 8:19 NIV).

A friend of mine once mentioned that she would like to see a dolphin. We were sitting by the ocean on a cliff face, and I turned to her, full of faith, and stated matter of factly, "We have the authority to summon the dolphins." Then I declared, "Dolphins come." We sat looking down at the ocean below. Within a few short minutes, a pod of dolphins appeared before our eyes. God loves to reveal himself, a loving Father who loves to give good gifts to His children. This was a gift, and our hearts were full of gratitude that He would give us the desires of our hearts. Those are the moments we reside in our identity, the times when we get to co-create with the God of the Universe, the One who is the Kingdom of Heaven, the One whom we live for.

More Lord

Daniel was thrown into the lions' den. Whilst He was there, it was the Lord that shut the lion's mouth. It was the Lord who was the hedge of protection around Daniel, ensuring that no harm would come up against Him. Daniel was a man acknowledged as a servant of God. This is the tangible reality of walking with God and being surrounded by His presence. He was in the very center of darkness, a place that I imagine would instill fear and anxiety in most people, yet His perspective was fixed upward, aware of the spiritual realm, that a ministering angel was in His presence shutting the mouths of the lions.

> *At the first light of dawn, the King got up and hurried to the lions' den. When he came near the den, he called to Daniel in an anguished voice, "Daniel, servant of the living God, has your God, whom you serve continually, been able to rescue you from the lions?" Daniel answered, "May the King live forever! My God sent his angel, and he shut the mouths of the lions. They have not hurt me, because I was found innocent in his sight. Nor have I ever done any wrong before you, Your Majesty* (Daniel 6: 19–22 NIV).

Greater Things

When we partner with God, nothing is impossible! What does this look like? Shutting the mouth of lions, dispersing the rain, taking Goliath down. Can even entire principalities (spiritual rulers) of a region leave as we shift atmospheres with the Power of God?

I believe we have been given the authority to do that. Why don't we see it happening? It is by faith we cast out demons. (Hebrews 11) I think we overcomplicate things at times, making it so much bigger and often overwhelming. God's word says to seek first the kingdom and His righteousness and all these things will be added to you. His Kingdom is what we seek; His presence. I long to hear His voice, to seek the Kingdom of God, not a kingdom I have established in my head.

I long to live my life attuned to the awareness of Heaven. Slowing down in my day-to-day life and thinking about Him increases my awareness of God's presence, attuning my ear to Him. I have spent much of my life running from one activity to the next. This is chaotic and creates anxiety, the rush of adrenaline in moving from one activity to another.

What if I slowed down? What if I stopped every day and became aware of my thoughts? What if I became aware of what was occurring within me and around me? As I intentionally choose to slow down and become present in the moment, I am able to take the time to discern all that I am experiencing.

It is when I slow down that I begin to breathe deeply, calming my heart rate and seeing with greater clarity. When I choose to stop, take a walk out in nature, and be still, I receive clarity, peace, and beautiful alignment. It is in the slowing down that you notice the intricacies of God's designs with an increasing awareness of His hands at work. I appreciate the simple moments when I stop and am in awe, like seeing a water droplet sitting so delicately on top of the grass blade. We must choose to practice being still, slowing down with greater awareness.

Stop. Take a deep breath and become aware of your thoughts, aware of your body from your head to your toes. As you breathe in, recognize any tension you are carrying in your back, shoulders, neck, and head. At each breath, feel your body relax and tension lift. At each breath, say or think of a name or characteristic of God, for example, Yahweh, Elohim, Jehovah Jireh, holy, worthy, etc.

Whilst I mentioned many testimonies of shifting the weather, I believe that this translates into shifting the spiritual atmosphere. Both require faith, and both require partnership with God, acknowledging that He is the all-powerful One and I am in union with Him.

All glory must go to God for His love and faithfulness.

Activation: Holy Spirit, how can I partner with you to see your love and Power demonstrated on the Earth? Pray Ephesians 1:17–21 (NIV), *I keep asking that the God of our Lord Jesus Christ, the glorious Father, may give you the Spirit of Wisdom and Revelation, so that you may know Him better. I pray that the eyes of your heart may be enlightened so that you may know the hope to which He has called you, the riches of His glorious inheritance in His holy people, and His incomparably great power for us who believe. That power is the same as the mighty strength he exerted when he raised Christ from the dead and seated Him at His right hand in the heavenly realms, far above all rule and authority, power and dominion, and every name that is invoked, not only in the present age but also in the one to come.*

Linger and Listen: Allow God to speak to you about His power, love, wisdom, and revelation.

Ask Jesus: What does it look like to live a life of faith?

Chapter 14

THE VINE AND BRANCHES

I have spoken much about the importance of co-laboring with God. The Lord is so kind and intentional in choosing us to work with Him. He doesn't have to use us, and yet it is His delight to partner with His children.

In the previous chapters, I have addressed discernment and our response in shifting atmospheres. Here, I want to emphasize that the responsibility is not on your shoulders! This may seem contradictory to what I have said previously, but we must understand that at the core of all of it, the Lord God Almighty is the One working. It is through remaining in Him and Him remaining in us that we will bear fruit. It is God we petition to and ultimately determines how things play out, what happens, and when. It is God who shifts the atmosphere, moved by our intercessory prayers. And it is God who answers those prayers. Healing, life, restoration, and peace are released from Him. It is His breath, the breath of life, that breaks chains and sets people free. It is the Lord's heartbeat to see His children restored back to intimacy with Him. The Lord desires to see His children saved, healed, and delivered.

Union/Co-laboring with Him

When we live with the revelation that we are One with God, things that seem impossible immediately become possible, and the supernatural becomes our normal. What would it look like to recognize that I no longer live, but Christ lives in me? If the very power that raised Christ from the dead lives in me, then I, too, must acknowledge there must be more than just being saved. Jesus didn't just die to make sure we did not go to hell but to restore us back to an intimate relationship with the Father. He loves to co-labor with us in a beautiful, divine partnership with Him for us to remain in Him and He in us. He longs for connection, for intimacy to walk with us in the cool of the day. He loves us so much that he sent a helper to live inside of us. He cannot get any closer to us than He already is. The very living God lives inside of us!

> *You are already clean because of the word I have spoken to you. Remain in me, as I also remain in you. No branch can bear fruit by itself; it must remain in the vine. Neither can you bear fruit unless you remain in me. I am the vine; you are the branches. If you remain in me and I in you, you will bear much fruit; apart from me you can do nothing* (John 15: 3–5 NIV).

I lay in my hammock outside in my backyard one day, sheltered by a grapevine that was delicately draped over a wooden roof structure. As I began observing it, I was struck by how similar the vine and branch were to one another; in fact, I could not distinguish between them. Like fingers interlaced when a couple holds hands, Jesus is one with us, and we cannot be separated from His presence, for He is in all things. When I am in union with Him, His blood pumps through my veins. Jesus has given us a command to remain in Him, and He will remain in us. We bear fruit when we remain in Him. Our sustenance, nourishment, and life come from the vine, from Him. We are one with Him. Let's begin to live like we are one.

My life verse, a verse that I pray daily:

Not to us, Lord, not to us but to your name be the glory, because of your love and faithfulness (Psalm 115:1 NIV).

It is to Him! Any time He moves, the atmosphere shifts, lives are set free and altered, and we give all the glory to His name. All the credit is to go to His name, everything comes back to gratefulness and thankfulness to Him. I love the quote, "Whatever we have honor for, grows." I truly believe that each time we are thankful and bring honor back to His name, our gift grows, and so does our authority. Yet it was never ours to begin with, but the Lord's. By His grace, He gives us the gifts to bring glory back to His name. Each time He moves, He speaks, and He shifts; we get the privilege of having our hearts attuned to Him to praise and thank Him for all that He has done and all that He is. It blows my mind that every single time someone is set free, or the atmosphere shifts, a life truly is impacted; a life is changed. God is just so so good!

Let Me Build

I was sitting with the Lord and asked Him, "What is on your heart today, God?"

The Lord responded, "Let me build. Will you trust? Will you surrender? Will you let me build?" So often, we find ourselves reading more books and listening to more podcasts in search of answers when He is the answer. He is the one who builds all things. So, whilst I have shared insights that I have gained and strategies I have learned along the way, it is Jesus that builds. It is not our efforts, accomplishments, or the great things we have done. The God of grace and mercy gives good gifts abundantly. He teaches us how to sustain and grow. The gifts are from Him, and the gifts are for Him. The Lord has chosen us as His vessels. So let the Lord build. Attune your ear to Him, your heart affection and attention to Him, and allow Him to build in your life.

The Lord told me, "I am the brick, I am the hammer, I am the mortar, I am the builder, I am the light and you are my apprentice that I am raising up." Jesus said, "I only do what I hear my father doing." Everything is in obedience to His voice, His ways. I must know His voice, the most familiar voice I have experienced.

"Will you let me build?"

Activation: Repeatedly say out loud, "You are in me, and I am in you; you are the vine and I am the branch, we are one."

Linger and Listen: What areas in your own life is He saying to you; "Let me?" Allow Him to reveal areas where you must relinquish control and surrender.

Ask Jesus: Lord, you say, "Let me build." Reveal to me what you want to build in my life. I encourage you to pause and ask the Lord, "What does it look like to allow you to build?" You say, "Let me. " Teach me what that looks like. May the words resound in my spirit as He speaks a tender, loving whisper, "Let me build."

Chapter 15

HEART POSTURE

Is your heart positioned for success in God's purposeful gifting?

Is gratitude for His gift coupled with an eagerness to serve Him and see Him exalted?

Being aware of our heart posture (careful of pride and arrogance, taking credit, carrying burdens) is being forewarned of footholds the enemy searches for within us. I see it when I consider how I have shared a testimony and the word choice when giving myself credit. Absolutely nothing is mine; no credit ought to come to me. I don't deserve it, and nothing is owed to me. I can do nothing of my own accord as it always comes back to stewarding what He has given us and giving all the credit, thankfulness, and glory back to Him. Our hearts truly are the wellspring of life. I long for my heart to remain humble and with a pure heart that always seeks to keep Jesus at the center, to know all things are to Him, for Him, and from Him. It is *In Him that all things hold together* (Colossians 1:17 NIV). Everything exists in Him.

There are times we can get caught up in ourselves. We take on the responsibility, the burden, as if we are warring on our own. This leaves us lonely and exhausted. There have been days I wake so overwhelmed—feeling like it is all up to me. My body notices this first. My shoulders become heavy with tension, my jaw clenched, my heart beating faster, and I breathe in short, quick breaths from my chest rather than deep breaths from my lungs.

Pay attention to physiological responses because they are necessary clues that we are carrying what we should not. Everyone's response will look uniquely different. However, our baseline should be peace. A tangible peace that surpasses understanding and cannot be explained, a peace that seeps into every cell of our being. It releases tensions in our body, slows our heart rate, and calms our breath to recognize that the Prince of Peace has chosen to inhabit us– body, soul, and mind. I believe we must experience this physiological response to peace, and it is the result of a daily choice to behold the King of Kings and be overwhelmed by His goodness and presence.

We were never meant to do anything alone. We were never meant to fix the problem or be the solution. The Lord God Almighty is the One who has all power, authority, and dominion. We are simply His vessels.

> *Come to me, all you who are weary and burdened, and I will give you rest. Take my yoke upon you and learn from me, for I am gentle and humble in heart, and you will find rest for your souls. For my yoke is easy and my burden is light* (Matthew 11:28–30 NIV).

God is the God of rest. He is the one who takes our weariness and burdens. In a divine exchange, He gives us rest as we give Him our cares.

False Responsibility

When we get out of peace and experience the physical symptoms of it, we have taken on False Responsibility.

Often, we are not aware of this immediately. The sweet convictions of the Holy Spirit will reveal it to us or be revealed by the wisdom of those trusted people we have invited into our lives, such as mentors, leaders, family, and friends. Once we are aware, we have a responsibility to respond immediately. We take it and place it back at the feet of Jesus, a heart that is malleable, ever-changing, and transforming.

False responsibility is exhausting. It always leads me to strive. It says, "If I just do x, y and z then it'll all be better." It places requirements to strive harder, do more, think differently, pray more, fast more and do all the work, exert all of the energy because after all, if you are carrying all the responsibility you will live with the belief system that *you* are the Savior of the world. Even as I am writing this I feel sick to my stomach. It sounds so horrible to think that we would take on the world and think that we, ourselves, have sole responsibility to see change. With the mindset that you are the only one that can do it, of course, will create a sense of being stressed, exhausted, overwhelmed, and in desperate need of a break. We *can* recognize when we slip into this. It is subtle and destructive.

When we pick it up, False Responsibility latches on to you, clinging tight. It is time to brush it off. It can be as simple as doing a prophetic act of brushing or shaking it off your shoulders. You may feel the weight physically fall off. Those in your Kingdom community can pray over you; you can ask them to brush it off as well. Remember: the responsibility is not yours to take on. We are not meant to come under the weight of the atmosphere. Brush it off, and pop back up! Jesus has gained the victory, and His victory is our weapon.

Stop Everything

Be moved by God's heart for His children with a longing to see restoration, but know that you do not carry the weight or believe that you are the one responsible for seeing it happen.

When I recognize that I have taken on a responsibility that was not mine, I stop. I literally stop everything. I cannot emphasize how effective this is. To counteract "doing" is to simply be still with Him. Be still before Him in rest, in peace, perhaps in complete silence, or in the Word, or worshiping. Find something that you love to do and simply do it with Jesus. It could be the creative arts, hiking, swimming, going for a drive, or finding a spot to view the sunrise or sunset. Whatever it is, the goal is undivided attention with Him; an ear attuned to His voice; a time set aside to be with your best friend, your Lord and Savior. A heart posture aligned in praise and adoration of Him. I speak to Him and share who He is and who He is to me, and I look to Him as the answer to every problem and as the restorer. His plan is to restore all things!

Slow Down

Slowing down and stopping has been a helpful tool enabling me to become aware more quickly that I have stepped out of peace. It's in the slowing down that we recalibrate, receive His peace, and hear His voice clearly. In chaos and taking on False Responsibility, it is hard to hear the voice of the Holy Spirit. Slow down, be present and attentive to your heart and you will avoid becoming completely overwhelmed.

Activation: Read Colossians 1:16–17. Meditate on 'In Him'.

I encourage you to stop now, be still, and become aware of what you are feeling. Ask the Holy Spirit if there are any areas where you have taken on False Responsibility. In your hands, see any heaviness, striving, restlessness, or burdens you have chosen to carry. Picture Jesus in front of you and invite Him to come and take this from your hands. As you release it and allow Him to take it, become aware of your body, your breathing, and your mind. Watch as Jesus takes it from you and repent for the times you have taken this upon your shoulders.

Linger and Listen: Get outside in nature, be still before Him, and let Him speak.

Ask Jesus: How do I incorporate rest into my daily life?

Chapter 16

KNOWING THE FATHER'S HEART

I want to be moved by Abba's heart, to know Him more and more. We *must* know Him, see Him, and walk with Him. We cry out for His Kingdom to come on Earth as it is in Heaven, but there is the yearning to grow in wisdom and revelation of what that truly means. It is His Kingdom that we long to come and infiltrate every sphere of our lives, families, regions, and nations. To see the Kingdoms of this world become the Kingdom of our God. Whilst we can't truly grasp the magnificence of who He is, the all-knowing, all-powerful, all-glorious King of Kings, we have no power of our own accord but only the power and authority that has been given to us by Jesus Christ, the King of the Universe. He is worthy of all praise, glory, and honor. I feel so moved by my heart for Him to stop, to praise, and to worship Him.

> *Shout for joy to the Lord, all the Earth.*
> *Worship the Lord with gladness;*
> *come before him with joyful songs.*
> *Know that the Lord is God.*
> *It is he who made us, and we are his;*
> *We are his people, the sheep of his pasture.*
> *Enter his gates with thanksgiving and his courts with praise;*
> *give thanks to him and praise his name.*

For the Lord is good and his love endures forever;
His faithfulness continues through all generations
(Psalm 100:1–5 NIV).

Pause and Praise

I encourage you to pause and praise Him. A heart that praises Him not for what He has done, or what He can do but simply to praise Him for who He is, the Lord of the Universe; Jesus, Abba Father, the One who has loved us so dearly and so intimately that He sent His One and only Son to die on our behalf so that we may live; so that we could be restored to an intimate relationship with the Father, not as a distant God, but as a loving Father who holds our head against His chest, champions us, and loves us with an inexpressible, magnificent everlasting love. The Lord chooses to deposit gifts, talents, strengths, and weaknesses within us so that we can use all that we are and all He has created us to be for His glory.

Revealed in Jesus

With discernment, I believe we must understand the Father's heart. God's heart is revealed through Jesus. At the core God is the restorer. He is good, kind, merciful, faithful, and full of grace and love. Abba Father longs for His children to be set free, to know their identity as beloved, chosen, set-apart, and royal. We are justified and are no longer sinners, but rather saints made holy, righteous, pure, and spotless.

We must believe that God's heart is for us and not against us.

God's plans are to prosper us and not harm us (Jeremiah 29:11 NIV).

You no longer need to walk around believing that you are bound by sin, repeatedly communicating how bad you are, how much of a sinner you are, and how distant you are to God. No, we are God's children whom He loves and adores. We are His cherished sheep that He would do anything to find and nurture back to safety and healing. He does not bring pain and sickness to establish perseverance within us; that is not the God that I know. For it is the enemy that comes to steal, kill and destroy and it is the Lord that brings life and life abundance. When we grasp a glimpse of His heart, we can pray in the will of the Father, aligning with Him and seeing His Kingdom come. We get to partner with Jesus as He intercedes for us.

Jesus is one-third of the Trinity, and yet He still declares

> *Very truly I tell you, the Son can do nothing by himself; he can do only what he sees his Father doing, because whatever the Father does the Son also does. For the Father loves the Son and shows him all he does. Yes, and he will show him even greater works than these, so that you will be amazed* (John 5:19–20 NIV).

Jesus, the Son of God, the Savior of the world declares that He can do nothing Himself but only does what He sees His Father doing. Therefore, Jesus must see what His Father is doing; His eyes are enlightened to see what Abba Father is doing. It is spoken in the present tense, even now Jesus is doing what He sees His Father doing. He is intimate and so aware of His Father at all times. The Father shows Jesus all that He does.

If Abba Father reveals to Jesus all that he does, we, too, have been given access to see all that He does too. We must see God. Lord, may we see you rightly!

It Takes Just One

I have been thinking a lot lately about the impact we have on the world around us. It just takes one person who knows God. One who is faithful, one turned to the Lord, who cries out and intercedes on behalf of the people. Did you know that we can move the heart of the Father?

It is in connection and intimacy with Him that we move His heart. He is moved by our hearts when He "knows us."

I am reminded of Abraham in Genesis 18. I have been struck by the story where Abraham stopped and interceded on behalf of the people of Sodom. God declared that He had chosen Abraham.

> *For I have known (Yāḏa) him, in order that he may command his children and his household after him, that they keep the way of the LORD, to do righteousness and justice, that the LORD may bring to Abraham what He has spoken to him* (Genesis 18:19 NKJV).

Most versions say, "For I have *chosen* Him." Known/chosen: yāḏa

It is in the knowing that God's heart was moved by Abraham's request. Abraham cried out on behalf of the people, and God was moved and responded. God heard the cry, pleading and interceding. It was in a relationship, in the knowing that God heard, that He was moved and altered His decision. It was in the knowing that God responded. "For I have known Him."

In most versions, it says," I have *chosen* Him." Why are they interchangeable, both *known* and *chosen*? In knowing He has chosen, He is invited into a place in our hearts and minds where He is moved by our hearts' cry and impacted by our requisitions.

Abraham was a man of faith, a man who was known by God. A man who was hand-picked and chosen by God.

He moved God's heart.

When Abraham pleaded on behalf of the righteous people to be spared. Abraham moved God's heart, and there was a response as God spared Abraham's nephew Lot. As we see further in the story, it says,

> *"So when God destroyed the cities of the plain, he remembered Abraham, and he brought Lot out of the catastrophe that overthrew the cities where Lot had lived."* (Genesis 19:29 NIV).

Abraham was a man of faith. I don't know about you, but I long to be known by the Lord. I am chosen by Him. It is not a coincidence that He has chosen you; he has placed in your heart a people, a sphere of influence that you have the privilege to intercede on behalf of. We, too, can move God's heart. Can we all? I believe so, to walk, allowing Him to know you.

We have an eternity to gain revelation on the facets of God's heart. As we behold Him we become more and more like Him. We are fully equipped and armed with all the artillery for battle.

Will you go out and utilize discernment as a life-giving weapon?

Activation: Imagine yourself on the edge of the river of Living Water, stepping in, continuing to go deeper into the River of Life, a heart of adoration and worship. Be refreshed by the wind of refreshing.

Linger and Listen: Be vulnerable before the Lord. Allow Him to be known by you. As you invite Him into your heart, step into His heart, into the divine dance with Abba Father.

Ask Jesus: Abba Father, teach me your heart, your ways that I may know you and see you rightly. Would you give me divine strategies on how to utilize discernment as a life-giving weapon in my own life? Teach me what my role is Isaiah 61 mandates.

Conclusion

HEART OF THE MATTER

The goal in all of it is connection with the Holy Spirit. The gift of discernment goes hand in hand with intercession. I am constantly engaging with my heart and inviting the Holy Spirit, asking questions: What am I feeling? Was I feeling this earlier? Holy Spirit what are you revealing? Who is this for? What would you like me to do with this awareness?

Over the years, I have engaged with the Holy Spirit in what I felt and sensed and sought Him in what I ought to do with this knowledge. The more I engaged with the Holy Spirit the more my gift increased. It has been a sharpening, a clarity to discern. The sphere of influence grows, and it moves from discerning what an individual is feeling to corporately what is happening in an atmosphere, into discerning what I am feeling for a greater atmosphere, a town, a city, or even a nation.

Intimacy with Him

Throughout my journey, I am more convinced than ever that every encounter has the potential to lead to greater intimacy and connection with Abba Father. The beautiful thing is that we get to choose how affected or unaffected we are by the voice of God. He longs to speak to us! In fact, you have never not heard the voice of God; from the moment you were born, He has spoken to you whether you recognized it or not. The Holy Spirit gently whispers in the everyday mundane moments. Whether it is in Scripture, in conversation with others, through creative expression, during a walk, in nature, in dreams, in visions, or as something catches your eye, etc.

In all of it, God is always speaking and longing for even greater intimacy and encounters with His children.

My life has been a journey; one of faith, pain, triumph, and defeats. Yet, through it all, one thing that I know to be true: nothing in our journey is wasted; each moment is an invitation to lead us closer to the King.

Captivated by His Love

Over the expanse of a year, I continually saw the same vision; a beautiful vision where Jesus was down on one knee holding a rose as though He were proposing. Each time, I felt so loved and seen as though we were the only two in the world. Jesus is longing for our attention and our affection. When you radically love someone, you will do anything for them. Jesus is looking for laid-down lovers who will choose to surrender all to follow Him. I believe it begins with the simple moments of obedience. It is the greatest love story of all time! A love story so radical that one encounter with His love will change everything!

His love is the pinnacle; everything revolves around love, His love.

It is from the overflow of the Lord's love that I wrote this book. His gentle whispers have led me on a journey to long for more of Him and for the fountain of life to bubble out of me and impact the world around me. I long for everyone around me to have a tangible encounter with the One true God; The Way, the Truth, and the Life. Every day we can choose to have an ear attuned to Heaven, to walk confidently our identity and authority, to see His Kingdom come on Earth as it is in Heaven and as the Bride of Christ boldly profess the name of Jesus.

God has equipped us with all that we need to partner with Christ and bring the Kingdom of God to Earth. One day, every knee will bow and every tongue will confess that Jesus is Lord. Jesus is the answer, Jesus is the solution, and Jesus is everything.

If you have not personally experienced the love of God, I encourage you to stop right now and ask Jesus to reveal His love for you, then arise, and saturate the atmosphere with the transformational love of God.

ABOUT THE AUTHOR

Australian-born Alisa Polkingthorne's life has been one big adventure. From living in Southeast Asia to the United States and now in Sunshine Coast, Queensland, home of the 2nd Wonder of the Natural World, the Great Barrier Reef. But nothing compares to the adventure of discovering the powerful gift of shifting atmospheres through discernment and the wonders revealed to her by the spirit of Almighty God through Jesus Christ. She recently launched, Mitwa Ministries, directed at equipping believers to hear God's voice and to know their authority, gifts, and calling, and to walk confidently as God's beloved children, through intimacy with the Lord Jesus Christ.

"My heart beats for revival and to see individuals step into the fullness of who they are in Christ. I am utterly convinced that Jesus' love is tangible, bringing transformation, life, hope, forgiveness, healing, freedom, and restoration. I am here to share words that God has placed on my heart."

A former primary school teacher, Alisa hungered for more and found herself on the other side of the globe, at Bethel School of Supernatural Ministry in Redding, California, USA. It was there clarity came and her book, *Radiating Glory*, was birthed.

When she is not guiding others into the supernatural truths she's discovered, she is delighting in "the small things." "I enjoy moments to be still in nature, worshipping, spending time at the beach, hiking trails, at a local cafe, socializing, camping, pilates, and sports. I enjoy connecting and being part of a community." Alisa's passion for people is demonstrated in all she does. Find out more about Alisa and Mitwa Ministries at:

mitwaministries.com

www.ingramcontent.com/pod-product-compliance
Lightning Source LLC
Chambersburg PA
CBHW060402080526
44583CB00012B/435